THE ETERNAL WISDOM OF SANATANA DHARMA

A BRIEF INTRODUCTION TO IMPORTANT LITERATURE

DR. SACHIN MISHRA

Dedication

Dedicated to our eternal ancestral lineage, maternal lineage, all the Gurus, all the well-wishers, and all the lovers of eternal traditions.

ॐॐॐ

Contents

Contents

Contents

Contents

Prayer

"Om Bhur Bhuvaḥ Swaḥ Tat Savitur Vareṇyaṃ Bhargo Devasya Dhīmahi Dhiyo Yo Naḥ Prachodayāt"

"We meditate on the glory of the Creator; Who has created the Universe; Who is worthy of Worship; Who is the embodiment of Knowledge and Light; Who is the remover of all Sin and Ignorance; May the Divine enlighten our Intellect."

ᛩᛩᛩ

Gurur Brahmaa Gurur Vishnu, Gurur Devo Maheshvarah, Gurur Saakshaat Param Brahma, Tasmai Shri Gurave Namah.

The Guru is Brahma, the Guru is Vishnu, the Guru is Maheshwara (Shiva), The Guru is the Supreme Brahman itself, I offer my salutations to that revered Guru.

Note: These verses are often recited as a salutation or homage to the Guru, emphasizing the significance and reverence attributed to the teacher or spiritual guide in Hindu tradition.

ᛩᛩᛩ

Ganga tarang ramanīya jatā kalāpaṃ Gaurī nirantara vibhūṣita vāma bhāgaṃ

The Ganga with its beautiful waves flowing through its locks, Gauri (another name for Goddess Parvati) adorns the left side continuously.

Note: These verses depict the divine attributes of the river Ganga (Ganges) and the goddess Gauri (Parvati) in Hindu mythology. The verses highlight the beauty and adornment associated with them.

ᛩᛩᛩ

About The Author

Dr. Sachin Mishra (Full name Dr. Sachindra Nath Mishra) is the founder of the Center for Pollution Control (CPC), a partnership firm established in Varanasi for biomedical waste management in 2005. Later on, this partnership firm was converted into a company to expand its business in other areas, known as CPC POWER INDIA PVT. LTD. His vision was to transform Varanasi, and after 18 years of hard work, he succeeded in making Varanasi largely free from biomedical waste. Today, CPC POWER INDIA PVT. LTD. is one of the leading companies in the disposal of biomedical waste in Varanasi.

Dr. Sachin Mishra's journey started in 2005 when diseases like diarrhea and dengue were spreading in Varanasi, which was also developing as a medical hub. The waste from hospitals was being dumped in residential areas. When he laid the foundation of CPC POWER INDIA PVT. LTD. for Biomedical Waste Management, he faced many questions, but he stood firm in his commitment. His efforts have resulted in 80-90% of the hospitals in Varanasi being associated with CPC POWER INDIA PVT. LTD.

In addition to his work in biomedical waste management, Dr. Sachin Mishra has been involved in several other social and environmental causes. He founded Recyclo Power in 2020 to address the issue of plastic waste management and has been associated with the plastic-free India campaign. He also runs dozens of non-governmental organizations and has associations with various government organizations. He has worked on initiatives such as providing free food programs, environmental protection, solid waste management, employment for the poor, construction of happy schools, medical distribution programs, drinking water arrangements, and distribution of blankets. He has also planted over 5000 saplings and installed tree guards to protect 70% of the plants.

Dr. Sachin Mishra is actively associated with sports and players and tries to solve their problems quickly. He is currently taking care of Asha Boxing Academy and other academies and clubs under his protection while discharging his responsibilities as the Vice President of Uttar Pradesh Boxing Association. He believes in providing high-quality training to children from over 50 poor families so that they can participate in competitions against the country and abroad and bring medals and recognition to their country and city, Varanasi.

Dr. Sachin Mishra's work has been recognized and awarded by several national and international organizations. He has received awards such as the International Hindi Utsav Samman in Malaysia, Indonesia, Port Louis Mauritius, and Dubai, the Environment Excellence Award in Varanasi, News of ABP News Channel Awards presented by Editor Shri Raj Kishore Ji, Entrepreneur of the Year 2020 UP in Mumbai by Intercontinental Quality Award, Anmol Ratan in 2021, Icon of Asia in 2022, and Rashtriya Gaurav Samman 2022 for his outstanding service work.

Preface

I would like to proudly state that there is nothing in the world greater than the knowledge of Sanatan Dharma because every aspect of existence, from the earth to the sky, from life to death, from creation to destruction, is described in great detail in numerous scriptures that India possesses. No one in the world has this treasure trove of knowledge, and whenever we think about it, we feel proud that we are heirs to such vast spiritual knowledge and fortunate to be a part of this Sanatan culture.

Starting the Sanatan Dharma Institution: To pass on this legacy of Sanatan wisdom to future generations towards our duty through selfless actions, I had the idea of starting a Sanatan Dharma institution called "Brahmrashtra Ekam." Along with this, I also felt a duty-bound emotion to revive some of the lost practices and culture of Sanatan Dharma. With the encouragement and guidance of my parents, gurus, and other relatives and friends, the institution "Brahmarashtra Ekam" was established.

Several events and activities were started under the umbrella of this institution, which included the participation of many saints and spiritual leaders. However, there was still a sense of incompleteness, as if something was missing. For example, in one event related to Bhagavad Gita in a city, the mayor was asked by some journalists to comment on the Gita, and he said that the book Bhagavadgita is related to the birth and life of Lord Shri Krishna, it confirms that he had not read it yet. This made me realize that although many people were involved in our institution, the message of Sanatan Dharma was still not reaching everyone.

In conclusion, the institution "Brahmrashtra Ekam" was founded to preserve and pass on the knowledge of Sanatan Dharma to future generations and revive some of the lost practices and culture.

However, it became evident that more work needs to be done to reach a broader audience and spread the message of Sanatan Dharma to everyone.

The book that follows is a testament to the vision and dedication of the founder of "Brahmrashtra Ekam," who sought to preserve and promote the rich spiritual and cultural heritage of India. Through the pages of this book, the reader will gain insights into the ancient wisdom of Sanatan Dharma, and discover how this timeless tradition continues to resonate with people around the world. The author takes the reader on a journey through the history, philosophy, and practices of Sanatan Dharma, exploring its key concepts and teachings in a way that is accessible and engaging. With its blend of scholarship and spirituality, this book offers a unique perspective on one of the world's most enduring and influential spiritual traditions.

Dr. Sachin Mishra
N-11/99-L-Plot No.8, Shivrajnagar Extn.
Ranipur, Varanasi - 221 010
Varanasi, Uttar Pradesh (India)

ॐॐॐ

VEDAS

ONE
INTRODUCTION TO VEDAS

The Vedas are a collection of ancient religious texts that originated in the Indian subcontinent. They are considered to be the oldest sacred scriptures of Hinduism and are believed to have been composed between 1500 and 1000 BCE. The Vedas are composed in Vedic Sanskrit and consist of four main texts - the Rigveda, Yajurveda, Samaveda, and Atharvaveda. These texts are further divided into various hymns, chants, and prayers.

The Rigveda is the oldest of the four Vedas and is composed of 1028 hymns in praise of various deities. It is believed to have been written around 1500 BCE and is the most important of the four Vedas. The Rigveda is divided into ten books, known as mandalas, and contains hymns in praise of various deities such as Agni, Indra, and Soma.

The Yajurveda is a collection of rituals and sacrifices that were performed during the Vedic period. It is divided into two main parts - the Shukla Yajurveda and the Krishna Yajurveda. The Shukla Yajurveda is written in prose and contains the mantras that were recited during the sacrifices, while the Krishna Yajurveda is written in a mix of prose and verse.

The Samaveda is a collection of chants and hymns that were sung during various Vedic rituals. It is believed to have been compiled around 1000 BCE and is divided into two main parts - the Purvarchika and the Uttararchika. The Purvarchika contains hymns that were sung during the Soma sacrifice, while the Uttararchika contains hymns that were sung during other Vedic rituals.

The Atharvaveda is the youngest of the four Vedas and is believed to have been composed around 1000 BCE. It contains hymns, spells, and incantations that were used for various purposes such as healing, protection, and attracting love. The Atharvaveda also contains hymns in praise of various deities such as Indra and Agni.

The Vedas were passed down orally from generation to generation for many centuries before they were eventually written down. The Vedas were considered to be the ultimate authority on religious and social matters in ancient India and were consulted for guidance on matters such as marriage, sacrifice, and worship.

The Vedas played an important role in the development of Hinduism and were instrumental in shaping the religious beliefs and practices of ancient India. They were also influential in the development of other religions such as Buddhism and Jainism.

In conclusion, the Vedas are an important part of ancient Indian history and have played a significant role in shaping the religious and social fabric of India. They continue to be an important source of knowledge and inspiration for millions of people around the world today.

ॐॐॐ

TWO
RIGVEDA

The Rigveda is one of the oldest and most important religious texts of Hinduism, composed in Vedic Sanskrit. It is considered the oldest of the four Vedas, which are the foundational texts of Hinduism. The Rigveda is believed to have been composed between 1500-1200 BCE and contains a collection of hymns, prayers, and mantras that were used in Vedic rituals.

The Rigveda is divided into ten mandalas or books, with each mandala further divided into hymns or suktas. The first mandala is the largest, containing 191 hymns, while the tenth mandala contains the smallest number of hymns, with only 191 hymns in total. Each hymn in the Rigveda is addressed to a specific deity or deities and is often accompanied by a description of the deity's attributes and powers.

The Rigveda contains hymns dedicated to various gods such as Indra, Agni, Soma, Varuna, and Vishnu. Indra, the god of thunder and war, is the most frequently mentioned god in the Rigveda, while Agni, the god of fire, is the second-most mentioned. The hymns of the Rigveda are also noted for their references to nature, with descriptions of rivers, mountains, and other natural features.

The Rigveda was transmitted orally for centuries before it was eventually written down, and its content and style reflect the religious and social customs of the time in which it was composed. It provides a unique window into the beliefs and practices of ancient Indian society and has played an important role in the development of Hinduism.

The Rigveda was not only used for religious purposes but also served as a source of knowledge and inspiration for other aspects of life, including medicine, agriculture, and politics. It contains verses on topics such as marriage, childbirth, social and moral behavior, and the role of kings and rulers.

The Rigveda has had a profound influence on Indian culture and society, shaping the religious, philosophical, and cultural traditions of the country. Its teachings and principles have also been incorporated into other religions such as Buddhism and Jainism, which have their roots in India.

In conclusion, the Rigveda is a rich and complex text that provides a valuable insight into ancient Indian society and religion. It is an important part of Hinduism and has had a significant impact on the development of Indian culture and civilization. Its hymns and teachings continue to inspire millions of people around the world today.

THREE
YAJURVEDA

The Yajurveda is one of the four Vedas, the foundational texts of Hinduism. It is believed to have been composed between 1200-1000 BCE and is written in Vedic Sanskrit. The Yajurveda is a collection of ritual formulas and mantras that were used in Vedic sacrifices and other religious ceremonies.

The Yajurveda is divided into two parts, the Shukla Yajurveda and the Krishna Yajurveda. The Shukla Yajurveda is also known as the "White Yajurveda" and is considered the older of the two versions. It contains hymns and mantras that are used in public sacrifices and rituals. The Krishna Yajurveda, on the other hand, is also known as the "Black Yajurveda" and contains the same hymns and mantras as the Shukla Yajurveda but in a different arrangement. It is used in private sacrifices and rituals.

The Yajurveda is unique among the Vedas in that it contains a prose section known as the Brahmana, which provides detailed instructions on the performance of Vedic rituals. The Brahmana also contains stories, legends, and mythological accounts related to Vedic deities and other religious practices.

The Yajurveda contains hymns and mantras dedicated to various gods such as Agni, Indra, and Soma. It also contains verses related to ethical and moral values, such as the importance of truth, honesty, and charity. The Yajurveda also provides information on important social and cultural practices such as marriage, childbirth, and funeral rites.

The Yajurveda played an important role in shaping Vedic religion and was central to the performance of Vedic sacrifices and other religious rituals. The mantras and hymns contained in the Yajurveda were believed to have the power to invoke the blessings of the gods and to bring prosperity and good fortune to those who performed the rituals correctly.

The Yajurveda has also had a significant impact on Indian culture and society. It has influenced the development of other Indian religious traditions such as Buddhism and Jainism, and has been a source of inspiration for poets, philosophers, and scholars throughout history.

In conclusion, the Yajurveda is an important text in the Hindu religious tradition and has played a significant role in shaping Indian culture and society. Its mantras, hymns, and teachings continue to inspire and guide millions of people around the world today.

ॐॐॐ

FOUR
SAMVEDA

The Samaveda is one of the four sacred texts of Hinduism, known as the Vedas. It is believed to have been composed between 1200-1000 BCE, making it one of the oldest religious texts in the world. The Samaveda is primarily a collection of hymns that are chanted during Hindu rituals, including the performance of sacrifices.

The name "Samaveda" comes from the Sanskrit words "sama," which means "melody" or "song," and "veda," which means "knowledge." This reflects the fact that the Samaveda is essentially a collection of musical compositions. The hymns in the Samaveda are derived from the Rigveda, but they are arranged differently and set to music.

The Samaveda is divided into two main parts: the Purvarchika and the Uttararchika. The Purvarchika contains hymns that are used in the first part of the Soma sacrifice, while the Uttararchika contains hymns that are used in the second part of the sacrifice.

The Samaveda is notable for its use of a musical notation system known as the "svara," which is used to indicate the melody and rhythm of the hymns. This system of notation is believed to have been the precursor to the modern Indian classical music system.

The hymns in the Samaveda are dedicated to various deities, including Agni, Indra, Soma, and the Asvins. The hymns praise the qualities and attributes of these gods, and seek their blessings and protection. Many of the hymns also contain philosophical and ethical teachings, such as the importance of living a virtuous life and practicing self-control.

The Samaveda has had a significant influence on Indian culture and society. Its musical compositions have been performed and studied for thousands of years, and have inspired countless musicians and poets. The Samaveda's teachings on ethics and morality have also played an important role in shaping Hindu philosophy and religious thought.

In conclusion, the Samaveda is a vital component of the Hindu religious tradition, providing a rich source of musical compositions and spiritual teachings. Its influence on Indian culture and society has been profound, and its impact can still be felt today. The Samaveda's unique musical notation system, philosophical teachings, and devotion to the gods make it a fascinating and valuable part of human history.

ॐॐॐ

FIVE

ATHARVA VEDA

The Atharvaveda is one of the four sacred texts of Hinduism, known as the Vedas. It is believed to have been composed between 1200-1000 BCE, making it one of the oldest religious texts in the world. The Atharvaveda is unique among the Vedas, as it contains a wide variety of content, including hymns, spells, incantations, and philosophical teachings.

The name "Atharvaveda" comes from the Sanskrit words "atharva," which means "fire priest," and "veda," which means "knowledge." This reflects the fact that the Atharvaveda was traditionally associated with the Atharvans, a group of priests who specialized in performing fire sacrifices.

The Atharvaveda is divided into 20 books, which contain over 700 hymns and spells. These hymns and spells are dedicated to various deities, including Indra, Agni, and Vishnu, as well as to abstract concepts such as Truth and Knowledge. The hymns are believed to have been recited during religious rituals, while the spells and incantations were used for a variety of purposes, including healing, protection, and warding off evil spirits.

One of the unique features of the Atharvaveda is its emphasis on domestic and personal rituals, as well as on magic and divination.

The text contains numerous spells and incantations designed to address everyday problems, such as sickness, infertility, and marital discord. It also contains detailed instructions for performing various rituals, such as those associated with childbirth, marriage, and death.

The Atharvaveda also contains important philosophical teachings, such as the concept of karma and the importance of dharma, or righteous living. The text stresses the importance of living a moral and ethical life, and the consequences of not doing so. It also includes discussions on various philosophical and metaphysical topics, such as the nature of the universe and the soul.

Despite its importance, the Atharvaveda was not widely accepted by orthodox Hindus until much later. This is because the text contains many spells and incantations that were seen as unorthodox or even taboo. However, the Atharvaveda eventually came to be recognized as an important part of the Hindu canon, and its teachings continue to influence Hindu philosophy and religious practice to this day.

In conclusion, the Atharvaveda is a rich and diverse text that provides a unique glimpse into ancient Hindu culture and religion. Its emphasis on domestic and personal rituals, as well as on magic and divination, sets it apart from the other Vedas. The Atharvaveda's teachings on ethics, morality, and metaphysics continue to shape Hindu thought and practice, making it an essential component of the Hindu religious tradition.

ॐॐॐ

VEDANGA

SIX
VEDANGA

Vedanga, meaning "limbs of the Veda," is a term used to refer to six auxiliary disciplines that were developed to aid the study and understanding of the Vedas, the ancient Hindu scriptures. These disciplines are believed to have been developed during the period of the late Vedic period, between 600 BCE and 200 BCE, when the Vedic texts were being compiled and organized.

The six Vedangas are Shiksha (phonetics), Kalpa (ritual), Vyakarana (grammar), Nirukta (etymology), Chandas (metrics), and Jyotisha (astronomy and astrology). Each of these Vedangas plays an important role in understanding the meaning, structure, and pronunciation of the Vedic texts.

Shiksha, or phonetics, deals with the proper pronunciation of the Vedic mantras. It teaches the proper articulation of the sounds of the Sanskrit language, including the proper pronunciation of vowels, consonants, and accentuation. Shiksha also teaches the proper use of the three musical accents used in the Vedic chanting, which are udatta (high tone), anudatta (low tone), and svarita (circumflex tone).

Kalpa, or ritual, deals with the proper performance of Vedic rituals and ceremonies. It provides detailed instructions on how to perform various Vedic sacrifices, including the use of the Vedic altar, the proper arrangement of the sacrificial fire, and the proper offering of the sacrificial oblations. Kalpa also deals with other aspects of Vedic ritual, such as the proper performance of funeral rites and the construction of altars and sacrificial implements.

Vyakarana, or grammar, deals with the structure and meaning of the Vedic mantras. It provides a comprehensive system of rules and principles for the analysis of the Sanskrit language, including the rules of declension, conjugation, and syntax. Vyakarana is essential for understanding the proper meaning of the Vedic texts, as well as for the interpretation of other Sanskrit texts.

Nirukta, or etymology, deals with the meaning and derivation of Vedic words. It provides a detailed analysis of the meanings of Vedic words, as well as their origin and derivation. Nirukta is important for understanding the symbolism and hidden meanings of the Vedic mantras, as well as for the interpretation of other Sanskrit texts.

Chandas, or metrics, deals with the structure and rhythm of the Vedic mantras. It provides a system of rules and principles for the analysis of the Vedic meters and their constituent parts. Chandas is essential for understanding the musical and rhythmic aspects of the Vedic mantras, as well as for the interpretation of other Sanskrit texts.

Jyotisha, or astronomy and astrology, deals with the study of the movement of the celestial bodies and their influence on human life. It provides a detailed analysis of the Vedic calendar and its astronomical basis, as well as the principles of astrology and horoscopy. Jyotisha is important for understanding the relationship between the movements of the celestial bodies and the events of human life, as well as for the prediction of future events.

In conclusion, the Vedangas are an essential component of the

Vedic tradition, providing a comprehensive system of rules and principles for the study and understanding of the ancient Hindu scriptures. Each of the six Vedangas plays a unique and important role in the analysis and interpretation of the Vedic texts, as well as in the performance of Vedic rituals and ceremonies. The Vedangas continue to be studied and practiced by scholars and practitioners of the Vedic tradition, ensuring the preservation and continuation of this ancient and rich cultural heritage.

ᐅᐅᐅ

SEVEN

SHIKSHA (PHONETICS)

Shiksha is one of the six classical disciplines of Vedanga, a group of auxiliary studies related to the Vedas. Shiksha deals with the study of phonetics, pronunciation, accentuation, and meter of Vedic texts. It is considered an essential tool for understanding and reciting the Vedas accurately, as even a slight deviation in pronunciation or accentuation can change the meaning of the words.

The term "Shiksha" comes from the Sanskrit root word "shiksh," which means to learn or teach. The word also has connotations of being pleasant and easily understood without mistakes. Thus, Shiksha emphasizes the importance of correct pronunciation and accentuation to ensure that the Vedic texts are not only recited accurately but also understood easily and correctly.

Shiksha is traditionally considered to have been authored by the sage Panini, who is also credited with writing the Sanskrit grammar text, the Ashtadhyayi. The Shiksha text is believed to date back to around the 5th century BCE, making it one of the oldest surviving texts on phonetics and pronunciation in the world.

The Shiksha text is divided into six chapters, each of which deals with a different aspect of phonetics and pronunciation. The first chapter discusses the importance of proper pronunciation and accentuation, while the second chapter covers the different organs of speech and their roles in producing various sounds. The third chapter deals with the different types of vowels and consonants, and the fourth chapter explains the rules of sandhi, or the combining of sounds in speech. The fifth chapter covers the different meters used in Vedic poetry, while the final chapter deals with the pronunciation of Vedic accents.

In addition to providing guidance on pronunciation and accentuation, Shiksha also includes discussions on the spiritual significance of sound and speech. It emphasizes the importance of sound in Hindu philosophy, with the belief that sound has the power to create and destroy. The text also explains how the recitation of Vedic mantras with proper pronunciation and accentuation can bring spiritual benefits and lead to liberation.

Shiksha remains an essential tool for students of the Vedas and is still taught in traditional schools and universities in India. It has also influenced the development of modern linguistics and phonetics, with many of its concepts and ideas still relevant today. The text's emphasis on the importance of sound and pronunciation has also led to the development of various chanting and musical traditions in India.

ᐅᐅᐅ

EIGHT
KALPA (RITUAL)

Kalpa is one of the six traditional disciplines of Vedanga, which are considered to be the ancillary texts that support the understanding and proper interpretation of the Vedas. Specifically, Kalpa deals with the rituals and procedures associated with Vedic worship and sacrifice. The word "Kalpa" means "procedure" or "ritual," and it provides a detailed framework for the performance of Vedic sacrifices and other religious practices.

The Kalpa texts are among the oldest known treatises on Vedic ritual practices and are considered to be an essential tool for the performance of the rituals themselves. The texts include detailed instructions on the construction of altars, the preparation of offerings, the recitation of mantras, and other aspects of Vedic worship. They also provide guidance on the timing and sequencing of the various ritual actions, as well as rules and regulations regarding the participants and their roles in the ceremony.

The Kalpa texts are divided into two major categories: the Shrauta Sutras and the Grihya Sutras. The Shrauta Sutras deal with the larger, more complex Vedic sacrifices, while the Grihya Sutras deal with domestic rituals and practices, such as birth ceremonies, weddings, and funerals.

The Shrauta Sutras provide detailed instructions on the construction of the ritual altar, the preparation of the sacrificial fire, and the offering of various substances to the gods. They also include information on the performance of specific rituals, such as the Agnihotra, the Soma sacrifice, and the Ashvamedha. These sacrifices were performed by the kings and wealthy families to obtain divine blessings and ensure their prosperity and success.

The Grihya Sutras, on the other hand, deal with domestic rituals and practices, such as marriage ceremonies, child naming ceremonies, and funerary rites. They provide guidance on the rituals and procedures associated with these events, as well as instructions on the proper conduct of daily life, including diet, cleanliness, and moral behavior.

In addition to the Shrauta Sutras and Grihya Sutras, the Kalpa texts also include a third category known as the Dharma Sutras. These texts provide guidance on the ethical and moral conduct of individuals and society as a whole. They include detailed instructions on the performance of duties and responsibilities based on one's social status, as well as laws and regulations regarding marriage, inheritance, and other aspects of daily life.

The Kalpa texts remain an essential tool for the performance of Vedic rituals and practices and are still studied and taught in traditional schools and universities in India. They have also influenced the development of Hinduism and other Indic religions, as well as the wider cultural and philosophical traditions of India. The texts' emphasis on proper ritual procedure and ethical behavior continues to be an important aspect of Hindu culture and spirituality.

ॐॐॐ

NINE

VYAKARANA (GRAMMAR)

Vyakarana, also known as grammar, is one of the six Vedangas, or auxiliary disciplines, of the ancient Indian scriptures called the Vedas. Vyakarana focuses on the study of language, specifically on the principles that govern the structure and usage of words and sentences. It is an important field of study in Indian philosophy and has been developed and refined over the centuries.

The origin of Vyakarana can be traced back to the ancient Vedic period, when the Vedas were being transmitted orally from generation to generation. The early Vedic texts were composed in a highly poetic and archaic language, which was difficult for the ordinary people to understand. This led to the development of a system of phonetics and grammar to ensure the accurate pronunciation and interpretation of the Vedic hymns. This system was further developed and refined over the centuries, leading to the emergence of different schools of grammar.

The earliest known grammar text is the Aṣṭādhyāyī, written by the ancient Indian grammarian Pāṇini in the 4th century BCE. The Aṣṭādhyāyī is a comprehensive and systematic treatise on Sanskrit grammar, consisting of 3,959 rules organized into eight chapters. It is considered one of the most influential works in the history of linguistics and has had a profound impact on the study of language in India and beyond.

The Aṣṭādhyāyī is based on a set of underlying principles and concepts, known as the sūtras, which are short, aphoristic statements that encapsulate the rules of grammar. The sūtras are organized into a hierarchical system, with the higher-level rules building on the lower-level ones. This system is highly logical and allows for the generation of an infinite number of sentences from a finite set of rules.

One of the key features of the Aṣṭādhyāyī is its focus on the internal structure of words, rather than their external form. Pāṇini recognized that many words in Sanskrit are composed of smaller units, called roots and affixes, which can be combined in different ways to generate new words. He developed a system of rules for combining roots and affixes, known as the sandhi rules, which allow for the formation of complex words and sentences.

Another important feature of the Aṣṭādhyāyī is its emphasis on the function of words in sentences, rather than their isolated meaning. Pāṇini recognized that the meaning of a word can change depending on its context, and developed a system of rules for analyzing the different functions of words in sentences. This system, known as the kāraka system, identifies the different roles that words can play in a sentence, such as subject, object, and instrument.

The Aṣṭādhyāyī has been studied and commented upon by generations of scholars over the centuries, leading to the development of different schools of grammar. These schools have interpreted and applied Pāṇini's rules in different ways, leading to the emergence of different grammatical traditions. Some of the most influential schools include the Vyākaraṇa and Mīmāṃsā traditions.

The study of Vyakarana has had a profound impact on Indian philosophy and culture. It has been used to interpret and analyze the meaning of the Vedas and other religious texts, and has played a key role in the development of Indian literature and poetry. The principles of Vyakarana have also been applied in other fields, such as music, medicine, and astrology, demonstrating its wide-ranging influence on Indian thought.

In addition to the Aṣṭādhyāyī, there are other important texts in the field of Vyakarana. These include the Mahābhāṣya, a commentary on Pāṇini's work written by the grammarian Patañjali, and the Siddhāntakaumudī, a comprehensive text on Sanskrit grammar written by the grammarian Bhaṭṭoji Dīkṣita in the 17th century.

The study of Vyakarana was also influential in the development of linguistic theories outside of India. Scholars such as Ferdinand de Saussure and Noam Chomsky have drawn on the insights and methods of Vyakarana in their own work on linguistics. The study of Vyakarana continues to be an important area of research in India and around the world.

In conclusion, Vyakarana is a vital field of study in Indian philosophy and linguistics. Its principles and methods have had a profound impact on the interpretation of religious texts, the development of literature and poetry, and the analysis of language in general. The Aṣṭādhyāyī, along with other important texts, continues to be studied and commented upon by scholars in India and around the world, demonstrating the enduring importance of Vyakarana in the study of language and culture.

༄༄༄

TEN

NIRUKTA (ETYMOLOGY)

Nirukta, which means "etymology" in Sanskrit, is one of the six Vedangas, or limbs of the Vedas, which are considered to be the sacred scriptures of Hinduism. The study of Nirukta is concerned with the interpretation and explanation of difficult or obscure words found in the Vedas, the oldest and most important texts of Hinduism. The Nirukta is attributed to the ancient sage Yaska and is one of the earliest works of Sanskrit philology.

The Nirukta is a systematic and comprehensive work that provides an analysis of over 3,000 words found in the Rigveda, the oldest of the four Vedas. It is divided into three main sections: Naighantuka, Naigama, and Daivata.

The first section, Naighantuka, deals with the etymology of words that are difficult to understand because of their unusual composition or structure. It provides a method of breaking down complex words into their component parts and identifying their meanings.

The second section, Naigama, deals with the interpretation of words based on their usage in the Vedas. It provides guidelines for understanding the context in which words are used and the meanings that can be derived from them.

The third section, Daivata, deals with the interpretation of words based on their association with deities and other divine beings. It provides insight into the religious and mythological significance of the words found in the Vedas.

The Nirukta is an important work in the field of Sanskrit philology and is considered to be one of the foundational texts of Indian linguistics. It provides a methodical approach to the interpretation and explanation of difficult words, and its principles and methods have had a profound impact on the study of language and literature in India.

One of the key contributions of the Nirukta is its recognition of the importance of context in the interpretation of words. Yaska recognized that words cannot be understood in isolation but must be understood in relation to the broader context in which they are used. This insight has had a lasting impact on the study of language and literature in India and has influenced the development of hermeneutics and semiotics in the Western world.

The study of Nirukta is closely connected to the study of Vyakarana, or grammar, another of the six Vedangas. Vyakarana provides the rules for the correct usage of words, while Nirukta provides the guidelines for their interpretation and explanation. Together, these two disciplines form the basis of Sanskrit philology and have had a profound impact on the development of Indian thought and culture.

In conclusion, Nirukta is an important area of study in the field of Sanskrit philology. It provides a methodical approach to the interpretation and explanation of difficult words found in the Vedas and has had a profound impact on the development of Indian thought and culture. Its recognition of the importance of context in the interpretation of words has influenced the development of hermeneutics and semiotics in the Western world. The study of Nirukta, along with the other Vedangas, continues to be an important area of research in India and around the world.

❧❧❧

ELEVEN

CHANDAS (METRICS)

Chandas, also known as Vedic meter or Vedic prosody, is one of the six Vedangas or limbs of the Vedas, the sacred scriptures of Hinduism. It is concerned with the study of poetic meters and rhythm in the Vedas, which are composed in a variety of poetic forms.

The study of Chandas is essential for understanding the intricacies of Vedic poetry and is considered to be one of the most important branches of Vedic learning. It provides the rules and guidelines for the correct use of meter and rhythm in Vedic poetry, which is essential for its proper interpretation and appreciation.

The Chandas Shastra, which is the text that deals with Chandas, is a vast and complex work that contains detailed instructions on the different meters and rhythms used in Vedic poetry. It is believed to have been composed by various sages over a period of several centuries and is divided into four main sections: Gāyatrī, Uṣṇik, Anuṣṭubh, and Brhati.

The first section, Gāyatrī, is the most important and deals with the most commonly used meter in Vedic poetry. It is a verse of three padas, or feet, each containing eight syllables. The Gāyatrī meter is used extensively in the Rigveda, which is the oldest and most important of the four Vedas.

The second section, Uṣṇik, deals with a meter of four padas, each containing seven syllables. The Uṣṇik meter is used primarily in the Samaveda, which is a collection of hymns and chants used in Vedic rituals.

The third section, Anuṣṭubh, deals with a meter of four padas, each containing eight syllables. The Anuṣṭubh meter is used extensively in the Yajurveda, which is a collection of hymns and chants used in Vedic rituals.

The fourth section, Brhati, deals with a meter of four padas, each containing twelve syllables. The Brhati meter is used primarily in the Atharvaveda, which is a collection of hymns and chants used in Vedic rituals.

The Chandas Shastra also provides detailed instructions on the correct pronunciation and intonation of Vedic poetry, which is essential for its proper interpretation and appreciation. It recognizes the importance of the correct use of meter and rhythm in Vedic poetry and provides a framework for its interpretation and analysis.

The study of Chandas is closely connected to the study of other Vedangas, such as Vyakarana (grammar) and Nirukta (etymology), which provide the rules and guidelines for the correct usage and interpretation of words in Vedic poetry. Together, these disciplines form the basis of Vedic learning and have had a profound impact on the development of Indian thought and culture.

In conclusion, Chandas is an important area of study in the field of Vedic learning. It provides the rules and guidelines for the correct use of meter and rhythm in Vedic poetry, which is essential for its proper interpretation and appreciation. The Chandas Shastra is a vast and complex work that contains detailed instructions on the different meters and rhythms used in Vedic poetry. The study of Chandas, along with the other Vedangas, continues to be an important area of research in India and around the world, demonstrating the enduring importance of Vedic learning in the study of language, literature, and culture.

❦❦❦

TWELVE

JYOTISHA (ASTRONOMY AND ASTROLOGY)

Jyotisha, also known as Vedic astrology, is one of the six Vedangas or limbs of the Vedas, the sacred scriptures of Hinduism. It is concerned with the study of astronomy and astrology in the Vedic tradition, and provides the guidelines for the calculation and interpretation of celestial phenomena.

The study of Jyotisha is essential for understanding the Vedic worldview, which recognizes the close relationship between the movements of the celestial bodies and the lives of human beings. The Vedas recognize that the movements of the sun, moon, and planets have a profound impact on the natural world and on human affairs, and Jyotisha provides the tools for understanding and interpreting these phenomena.

The Vedanga Jyotisha is the oldest and most important text on Vedic astronomy and astrology, and is believed to have been composed around 1400 BCE. It is divided into three main sections: mathematical astronomy, horoscopy, and omens.

The first section, mathematical astronomy, deals with the calculation and prediction of celestial phenomena such as eclipses, equinoxes, and solstices. It provides the guidelines for the construction of the Vedic calendar, which is based on the movements of the sun, moon, and planets, and is used for timing religious festivals and rituals.

The second section, horoscopy, deals with the interpretation of the positions and movements of the celestial bodies in relation to an individual's birth chart. This section provides the guidelines for calculating and interpreting an individual's horoscope, which is believed to reveal information about their character, destiny, and life path.

The third section, omens, deals with the interpretation of natural phenomena such as thunder, lightning, and eclipses, which are believed to have significance for human affairs. This section provides the guidelines for interpreting these omens and understanding their impact on human affairs.

The study of Jyotisha is closely connected to the study of other Vedangas, such as Shiksha (phonetics) and Vyakarana (grammar), which provide the tools for understanding and interpreting the Vedic texts. Together, these disciplines form the basis of Vedic learning and have had a profound impact on the development of Indian thought and culture.

Jyotisha has been an important area of study in India for thousands of years, and continues to be a vibrant and dynamic field of research and practice. While some critics argue that astrology has no scientific basis and is purely a matter of superstition, others argue that it provides a valuable framework for understanding the relationship between the movements of the celestial bodies and human affairs.

In conclusion, Jyotisha is an important area of study in the field of Vedic learning. It provides the guidelines for the calculation and interpretation of celestial phenomena, and offers a framework for understanding the close relationship between the movements of the celestial bodies and human affairs. The Vedanga Jyotisha is the oldest and most important text on Vedic astronomy and astrology, and continues to be a valuable resource for scholars and practitioners alike. The study of Jyotisha, along with the other Vedangas, continues to be an important area of research in India and around the world, demonstrating the enduring importance of Vedic learning in the study of language, literature, and culture.

UPANISHADS

THIRTEEN
UPANISHADS

The Upanishads are a collection of sacred Hindu texts that are considered to be among the most important philosophical and spiritual writings in the world. They form the final part of the Vedas, the ancient Indian scriptures that are the foundation of Hinduism. The Upanishads are written in Sanskrit and date back to around 800 BCE to 500 BCE.

The word "Upanishad" means "sitting down near" or "sitting close to" in Sanskrit. It refers to the practice of sitting close to a teacher to receive spiritual instruction. The Upanishads are a record of the conversations between the teachers and their students, and contain a wealth of philosophical and spiritual insights that are still relevant today.

There are over 200 Upanishads, but only 10 are considered to be the most important. These are known as the Principal Upanishads and include the Brihadaranyaka Upanishad, Chandogya Upanishad, Isa Upanishad, Kena Upanishad, Katha Upanishad, Mundaka Upanishad, Mandukya Upanishad, Prasna Upanishad, Svetasvatara Upanishad, and Taittiriya Upanishad.

The Brihadaranyaka Upanishad is one of the oldest and longest Upanishads, and it is believed to have been written around 800 BCE.

It contains discussions on various philosophical topics such as the nature of reality, the relationship between the individual and the cosmos, and the concept of Brahman.

The Upanishads explore many philosophical themes, including the nature of reality, the nature of the self, the relationship between the individual and the universe, and the nature of God. They also discuss the nature of karma, rebirth, and liberation.

One of the key teachings of the Upanishads is the concept of Brahman, which refers to the ultimate reality that underlies all of existence. Brahman is often described as being beyond description and beyond the limitations of time and space. It is said to be the source of all existence and the ultimate goal of spiritual practice.

Another important teaching of the Upanishads is the concept of Atman, which refers to the individual soul or self. The Upanishads teach that the Atman is identical to Brahman, and that realizing this identity is the key to spiritual liberation.

The Upanishads also discuss various spiritual practices, including meditation, yoga, and devotion. They emphasize the importance of cultivating spiritual awareness and developing a deep understanding of the nature of reality.

The teachings of the Upanishads have had a profound impact on Hinduism and on the broader spiritual and philosophical traditions of India. They have influenced the development of various schools of Hindu philosophy, including Advaita Vedanta, which emphasizes the unity of the individual soul and Brahman, and Yoga, which emphasizes the practice of meditation and spiritual discipline.

The Upanishads have also had a significant impact on the development of Buddhism and Jainism, two other major religions that emerged in India around the same time as Hinduism.

❦❦❦

FOURTEEN

ISHA UPANISHAD

The Isha Upanishad, also known as the Ishavasya Upanishad, is a concise yet widely studied text in Hindu philosophy. It forms part of the Shukla Yajurveda and is believed to have been written around 800 BCE, attributed to the ancient sage Yajnavalkya.

Comprising of 18 verses, the Upanishad is divided into two parts: the Shanti Mantra and the main text. The Shanti Mantra serves as a prayer for peace, while the main text delves into the nature of the self, the universe, and their interconnectedness.

The opening verse, "Isha vasyam idam sarvam yat kincha jagatyam jagat," expresses the belief that the Supreme Being pervades everything within the ever-changing universe.

The Upanishad emphasizes the concept of oneness and interconnectedness, asserting that Brahman, the ultimate reality, is present in all things. It teaches that the self, or Atman, is identical to Brahman and that realizing this unity leads to spiritual liberation.

The famous verse "Om Purnamadah Purnamidam" highlights the completeness and interdependence of all existence.

The Upanishad also addresses the concept of karma, emphasizing that actions have consequences and should be performed with detachment and selflessness.

Alongside its philosophical teachings, the Isha Upanishad offers practical guidance for leading a balanced and fulfilling life, advocating for the harmonization of material and spiritual pursuits, and living in harmony with nature.

For centuries, the Isha Upanishad has been revered by scholars and spiritual seekers for its profound insights into oneness, interconnectedness, detachment, and the pursuit of harmony. It continues to inspire individuals on their spiritual journeys.

ᮘᮘᮘ

FIFTEEN

KATHA UPANISHAD

The Katha Upanishad, an essential text within the Vedas, is renowned for its philosophical insights. Believed to have been composed around 300 BCE or earlier, it delves into profound questions about human existence, including the nature of the self, the relationship between the self and ultimate reality, and the path to spiritual liberation.

Structured as a dialogue between the young boy Nachiketa and the god of death, Yama, the Upanishad tells the story of Nachiketa's quest for knowledge. Nachiketa's questions revolve around the nature of the self, the afterlife, and the path to liberation.

Yama imparts profound wisdom in response to Nachiketa's inquiries. He reveals that the self is not the physical body or senses but the eternal Atman, which transcends death and change. Yama explains that virtuous deeds lead to a place of happiness in the afterlife, but even that realm is temporary and not the ultimate goal of existence. Yama further elucidates the path to liberation, emphasizing renunciation of desires and attachment, the importance of a spiritual teacher, and the practice of meditation and self-discipline to attain union with the divine.

The Katha Upanishad is renowned for its mantras, including the widely recited verse "Lead me from untruth to truth, from darkness to light, from death to immortality." It explores the nature of the divine and emphasizes that all of creation manifests the ultimate reality, Brahman.

In conclusion, the Katha Upanishad is a profound philosophical text that addresses fundamental inquiries about human existence. Its teachings on the self, the afterlife, and the path to spiritual liberation have had a lasting impact on Hindu philosophy and spirituality. The Upanishad remains revered and studied by scholars and practitioners worldwide.

ᑭᑭᑭ

SIXTEEN
KENA UPANISHAD

The Kena Upanishad is a significant philosophical text in Hinduism, part of the Sama Veda. It probes the nature of reality, the self, and the divine. The Upanishad begins with the question "By whom?" to prompt contemplation of the ultimate cause of existence. Its authorship and dating are uncertain but believed to be from the late Vedic period. The Upanishad comprises four sections with 35 verses, discussing the mind's limited role, the divine feminine Uma Haimavati, the transcendence of the ultimate reality, and the importance of seeking truth. It teaches that Brahman is the source of all existence, and knowledge, meditation, and self-realization are crucial for liberation. The Upanishad reveals the identity of the individual self (atman) with Brahman and stresses direct perception over intellectual understanding. Overall, the Kena Upanishad offers profound insights into reality, self, and spiritual attainment.

ৡৡৡ

SEVENTEEN

PRASHNA UPANISHAD

The Prashna Upanishad, part of the Atharva Veda, features six students asking questions to sage Pippalada on the nature of reality, self, and Brahman. Composed around the 1st millennium BCE, it explores profound concepts. The Upanishad begins with questions on creation, self-realization, dreams, deep sleep, prana (life force), and the ultimate reality. Pippalada provides insightful answers, revealing Brahman as the source of creation, the self as identical to Brahman, dreams as reflections of desires, deep sleep as a state of unity, prana as the bridge between body and self, and the ultimate reality as beyond words and concepts. The Prashna Upanishad also includes powerful mantras like the Gayatri mantra. It emphasizes meditation, introspection, and direct experience as pathways to understanding the ultimate truth.

ᗫᗫᗫ

EIGHTEEN

MUNDAKA UPANISHAD

The Mundaka Upanishad, a significant text in Vedanta, is widely studied in Hinduism. Part of the Atharva Veda, it consists of three chapters and explores the nature of the soul and the path to liberation. Written in Sanskrit around the 5th century BCE, its author is unknown but attributed to sage Shaunaka. The Upanishad distinguishes between lower knowledge (apara vidya) of the physical world and higher knowledge (para vidya) of the self and ultimate reality. It emphasizes the superiority of higher knowledge for attaining liberation. Describing Brahman as the source of creation, the second chapter portrays all existence as manifestations of Brahman. It outlines paths to realizing Brahman, such as meditation, knowledge, and devotion. The third chapter underscores the importance of a guru in spiritual realization, outlining the qualities a guru should possess and guiding seekers through a disciple-guru dialogue. The Mundaka Upanishad's teachings on the self and ultimate reality inspire spiritual seekers, influence Hindu philosophy, and its poetic language and metaphors make it a vibrant and timeless text.

ƿƿƿ

NINETEEN
MANDUKYA UPANISHAD

The Mandukya Upanishad is a concise yet profound text among the principal Upanishads. It delves into the nature of reality, consciousness, and the self, particularly in the Advaita Vedanta tradition. Named after Mandukya, founder of the Mandukya School of Hindu philosophy, it belongs to the Atharvaveda and consists of 12 verses divided into four chapters.

The first chapter explores the four states of consciousness: waking, dream, deep sleep, and pure consciousness (turiya). It asserts that the true self exists beyond these states, in a realm of pure consciousness.

The second chapter introduces Aum, the sacred syllable representing the ultimate reality. Aum symbolizes the universe's sound and source of creation, encapsulating all existence and signifying the goal of spiritual practice.

The third chapter analyzes Aum and its components—A, U, and M—associating each with different aspects of consciousness and stages of spiritual growth. Understanding the nature of Aum is believed to lead to liberation from the cycle of birth and death.

The fourth chapter establishes the identity between the individual self (jiva) and the ultimate reality (Brahman). It posits that they are not separate entities but different aspects of the same underlying reality.

The Mandukya Upanishad's profound exploration of existence and consciousness has solidified its place as a fundamental text in Hindu philosophy. Its teachings continue to inspire spiritual seekers and scholars alike, offering comprehensive insights into the nature of reality and the self.

༺༺༺

TWENTY

TAITTIRIYA UPANISHAD

The Taittiriya Upanishad, belonging to the Yajur Veda, is a principal Upanishad of Hinduism. Named after the Taittiriya school, it holds a significant place in Vedic learning. Composed around 500 BCE, it expounds upon the nature of the self, Brahman, and their interrelationship. This Upanishad is renowned for its detailed descriptions of meditation and spiritual practices.

Divided into three chapters, the first chapter, Siksha Valli, focuses on the pronunciation and teaching of Vedic mantras for spiritual purposes. The second chapter, Brahmananda Valli, delves into the nature of Brahman—the ultimate reality—and its connection to the individual self. The third chapter, Bhrigu Valli, features discourses on various meditation techniques and spiritual practices.

A well-known teaching from the Taittiriya Upanishad is the concept of the five sheaths (koshas) enveloping the individual self. These sheaths encompass the physical body, energy body, mental body, intellectual body, and bliss body. The Upanishad emphasizes that the goal of spiritual practice is to transcend these sheaths and realize the true essence of the self—pure consciousness.

The Upanishad provides detailed descriptions of various meditation practices, including the profound Om meditation. This practice involves focusing on the sacred sound of "Om" to attain realization of the ultimate reality. Additionally, the Upanishad discusses practices like yoga, self-inquiry, and devotion.

The Taittiriya Upanishad holds immense importance in Hinduism, influencing its philosophy and spirituality for centuries. It remains a revered text studied by spiritual seekers and scholars worldwide.

TWENTY-ONE
AITAREYA UPANISHAD

The Aitareya Upanishad is a major text in Hinduism, part of the Rigveda. It consists of three chapters and explores the creation of the universe, the nature of the self, and the ultimate reality of Brahman. It teaches that consciousness is Brahman and emphasizes the identity of the individual self with Brahman. The Upanishad describes the cosmology of the universe and discusses spiritual practices like meditation and sacrifice. It highlights the importance of self-realization and attaining liberation from the cycle of birth and death. The Aitareya Upanishad's teachings continue to inspire seekers on the path of spiritual realization.

TWENTY-TWO
CHANDOGYA UPANISHAD

The Chandogya Upanishad is a significant text in Hinduism, part of the Sama Veda. It consists of eight chapters and explores the nature of reality, the soul, and the relationship between the individual and Brahman. The Upanishad introduces sacred syllables and meditation methods to realize Brahman. It discusses the five elements and three states of consciousness. It describes the soul as eternal and explains the concept of reincarnation. The Upanishad explores different types of sacrifice and emphasizes the oneness of the individual soul with Brahman. It provides detailed instructions on meditation and highlights the importance of knowledge and the guru-student relationship. The Chandogya Upanishad's teachings offer profound insights into the nature of existence and continue to guide spiritual seekers.

ϷϷϷ

TWENTY-THREE
BRIHADARANYAKA UPANISHAD

The Brihadaranyaka Upanishad is an important and lengthy text in Hinduism. Divided into the Madhu Kanda and Muni Kanda, it explores topics such as the nature of reality, the self, and the significance of ritual and sacrifice. The dialogue between Yajnavalkya and Maitreyi is notable, emphasizing the pursuit of self-realization over material wealth. The Upanishad introduces concepts like reincarnation, karma, and the Gayatri mantra, which bestows wisdom and enlightenment. With over 6,000 verses, it offers profound philosophical insights and has influenced Hinduism and other religions. The Brihadaranyaka Upanishad remains a revered text for spiritual seekers worldwide.

PURANAS

TWENTY-FOUR
PURANAS

The Puranas are a collection of Hindu texts that convey the teachings and traditions of Hinduism. Written by the sage Vyasa, they are classified into Sattva, Rajas, and Tamas categories. The Puranas provide information about the gods and goddesses of Hinduism, their stories, relationships, and interactions with humans. They also offer instructions for religious practices. The Bhagavata Purana focuses on Vishnu, while the Shiva Purana focuses on Shiva. Other important Puranas include the Markandeya, Skanda, Matsya, and Varaha Puranas. These texts have influenced Hinduism and Indian culture, inspiring art, literature, and music. They continue to shape beliefs and practices, serving as a source of inspiration and guidance for millions.

ɔɔɔ

TWENTY-FIVE
BRAHMA PURANA

The Brahma Purana is an ancient Hindu text dedicated to Lord Brahma. It is divided into two parts: the Purvabhaga, which describes the creation of the universe and genealogy of gods and sages, and the Uttarabhaga, which focuses on the city of Prayaga and stories of Lord Vishnu and his avatars.

The first part explains the creation of the universe and the rituals to please the gods. The second part highlights the significance of Prayaga, its temples, and the importance of bathing in its rivers. It also narrates stories like the triumph of Prahlada over the demon Hiranyakashipu and Lord Vishnu's avatars such as Narasimha, Rama, and Krishna.

The Brahma Purana is renowned for its religious and mythological tales, exemplifying good triumphing over evil. Additionally, it covers scientific and social topics, including astronomy, medicine, and ethics. As a revered text in Hinduism, it is studied and recited by devotees seeking spiritual knowledge.

TWENTY-SIX
PADMA PURANA

The Padma Purana is one of the 18 major Mahapuranas of Hinduism, named after the lotus flower. It is an encyclopedic text composed in the 4th century CE. Divided into six books and numerous sections, it covers diverse subjects such as mythology, cosmology, philosophy, ethics, and rituals.

The Padma Purana narrates the creation of the universe and stories of gods and goddesses like Vishnu, Shiva, Brahma, and Devi. It includes legends of kings, sages, and their virtues. Ritualistic sections offer instructions on ceremonies, holy places, and festivals like Kumbh Mela and Diwali.

Devotion to God is a central theme in the Padma Purana, emphasizing worship, prayer, moral conduct, and the concept of karma. It also emphasizes dharma, highlighting societal duties, compassion, respect, and charity.

As a comprehensive text, the Padma Purana provides insights into Hindu mythology, philosophy, and religious practices. It has been revered by Hindus for centuries and continues to inspire and guide spiritual seekers today.

ᐅᐅᐅ

TWENTY-SEVEN
VISHNU PURANA

The Vishnu Purana is one of the major eighteen Puranas in Hinduism, dedicated to the god Vishnu. It was written by sage Parashara and is divided into six books.

The first book describes the creation of the universe, genealogy of gods, and their conflicts with demons. It also includes the story of the great flood and the subsequent re-creation of the world.

The second book focuses on the life and incarnations of Vishnu, such as Rama and Krishna. It explains the reasons for Vishnu's descent to earth.

The third book provides an account of solar and lunar dynasties of kings and the lives of sages and saints.

The fourth book explores cosmology, including astronomy, astrology, time, and the concept of karma and reincarnation.

The fifth book discusses religious practices and rituals, sacrifices, hymns, prayers, pilgrimage, and the different stages of life.

The sixth book covers topics related to the philosophy of Hinduism, including the nature of the self, the ultimate reality, and liberation or moksha. It includes stories of sages and their divine experiences.

The Vishnu Purana is a significant text in Hinduism, offering insights into mythology, philosophy, and religious practices. It is highly regarded and studied by millions of Hindus worldwide.

TWENTY-EIGHT
SHIVA PURANA

The Shiva Purana is one of the 18 Mahapuranas, ancient Hindu texts dedicated to Lord Shiva. It is composed of around 24,000 verses in seven books, covering various aspects of Shaivism.

The Vidyesvara Samhita focuses on the origin of the universe and the different forms of Lord Shiva. The Rudra Samhita is the largest section, containing stories of the creation of the universe, the gods, demons, and Lord Shiva's various forms and incarnations. The Shatarudra Samhita describes the ritual worship and recitation of the Shiva mantra. The Kotirudra Samhita centers on Lord Shiva's temples and the associated rituals. The Uma Samhita is dedicated to Parvati, Lord Shiva's wife, and narrates her birth and marriage to him. The Kailasa Samhita discusses the spiritual significance of Mount Kailash as Lord Shiva's abode. The Vayaviya Samhita contains stories of Lord Shiva's devotees and their spiritual journeys.

The Shiva Purana also imparts important teachings of the Shaivism tradition, emphasizing devotion to Lord Shiva, yoga, meditation, and the concepts of karma and reincarnation. It emphasizes leading a moral and virtuous life and striving for liberation or moksha.

One prominent story in the Shiva Purana is the churning of the ocean of milk, where gods and demons work together to obtain the nectar of immortality. During the churning, divine objects and beings emerge, and Lord Shiva drinks the deadly poison to save the universe, earning him the title of the world's savior.

In summary, the Shiva Purana is a significant Hindu text, providing insights into Shaivism's mythology and philosophy. It covers Lord Shiva's forms, incarnations, devotion, and the importance of spiritual practices. Esteemed by Hindus worldwide, it continues to guide and inspire their spiritual beliefs and practices.

ᗤᗤᗤ

TWENTY-NINE
BHAGAVATA PURANA

The Bhagavata Purana, also known as the Srimad Bhagavatam, is a revered Hindu scripture dedicated to Lord Vishnu, specifically his incarnation as Krishna. Written by sage Vyasa between the 8th and 10th centuries CE, it consists of twelve books and 18,000 verses. The main focus is on the life and teachings of Lord Krishna, including his birth, childhood, battles against demons, and ultimate return to his heavenly abode. The Bhagavata Purana also includes stories of other deities and teachings on yoga, morality, and the soul. It is considered an important scripture in the Vaishnavite tradition, providing spiritual guidance and inspiration. Translated into various languages, it has influenced religious practices and has been studied extensively by scholars and devotees. The Bhagavata Purana continues to be cherished and revered in Hinduism, offering profound insights into devotion and the path to divine connection.

THIRTY
NARADA PURANA

The Narada Purana is one of the eighteen major Puranas in Hinduism, believed to be compiled by Sage Narada. It is divided into two parts: Purva Khanda and Uttara Khanda. The Purva Khanda covers the creation of the universe and Lord Vishnu's manifestations, while the Uttara Khanda discusses dharma, the four varnas, yoga, devotion to Lord Vishnu, yugas, holy places, rituals, the Ganga river, the Mahabharata, and the worship of Lord Vishnu.

The Narada Purana emphasizes the importance of devotion, righteous behavior, and the consequences of sinful actions. It provides insights into Lord Vishnu's incarnations and highlights the significance of worshiping him for spiritual progress.

The scripture guides individuals to live virtuous lives and offers understanding of the universe's mysteries and their place within it. It is revered by Lord Vishnu's devotees and is recited in daily worship.

The Narada Purana is a valuable resource for those seeking a deeper understanding of Hinduism. Its timeless wisdom remains relevant and meaningful in the present day, resonating with people from various backgrounds.

❧❧❧

THIRTY-ONE

MARKANDEYA PURANA

The Markandeya Purana is one of the 18 major Puranas in Hinduism, composed of 137 chapters. It covers topics like cosmology, mythology, philosophy, ethics, and spirituality. Divided into five sections, it includes genealogies, creation myths, stories of deities, battles of the goddess Devi, tales of kings and sages, and discussions on yoga and liberation.

The Devi Mahatmya within the Markandeya Purana describes the battles of goddess Durga against the demon Mahishasura, and it is recited during Navratri. The story of King Harishchandra exemplifies the importance of truth and integrity.

The Markandeya Purana also explores philosophical concepts such as karma, dharma, and moksha, emphasizing righteous living and detachment. It provides insights into astronomy, geography, medicine, and rituals.

Overall, the Markandeya Purana is a comprehensive resource for Hinduism, offering knowledge of culture, mythology, and spirituality. It serves as a guide for those seeking a deeper understanding of Hindu traditions.

ॐॐॐ

THIRTY-TWO
AGNI PURANA

The Agni Purana is one of the eighteen major Mahapuranas in Hinduism, composed between the 8th and 11th centuries CE. Dedicated to the fire god Agni, it consists of 383 chapters and 15,000 verses.

This Purana emphasizes fire rituals and worship of Agni, providing detailed instructions on various sacrifices and yajnas. It explores different forms of Agni and covers topics like astrology, astronomy, and gemology. Descriptions of celestial bodies' movements and gem properties are included.

The Agni Purana delves into concepts of dharma, karma, and moksha, offering guidance for virtuous living and spiritual growth. It discusses the stages of life, the soul's nature, and the significance of meditation and yoga.

Legends and stories are also part of the Agni Purana, with a focus on Lord Shiva and his family. Tales like Shiva's marriage to Parvati, the birth of Kartikeya, and the churning of the ocean are included.

Overall, the Agni Purana serves as a valuable source for Hindu rituals, astrology, and spirituality. It emphasizes fire worship, provides knowledge on various subjects, and offers insights into leading a righteous life and attaining spiritual enlightenment.

༜༜༜

THIRTY-THREE

BHAVISHYA PURANA

The Bhavishya Purana is one of the major eighteen Puranas in Hinduism, believed to have been composed during the medieval period. It covers diverse topics such as history, geography, medicine, astrology, and religion. Divided into four parts, it consists of over 14,000 verses.

The first part narrates the creation of the universe, Lord Vishnu's incarnations (including Lord Krishna), and the Kurukshetra War. The second part focuses on the life of Lord Rama, his battles with demons, and the Ramayana epic.

The third part delves into astrology and prophecy, describing celestial phenomena, nakshatras (constellations), lunar days, and planetary significance. It includes prophecies about future events, including the appearance of Kalki, the final avatar of Lord Vishnu, in the Kali Yuga.

The fourth part provides insights into Hindu religion and culture, detailing rituals, worship practices, fasting, and festivals. It also covers different types of righteousness (dharma) and the four ages (yugas) of Hinduism.

The Bhavishya Purana is a revered text offering valuable knowledge about various aspects of life. Its prophetic nature and comprehensive coverage make it a significant resource for scholars and devotees in understanding Hinduism's history, culture, and spirituality.

ᐅᐅᐅ

THIRTY-FOUR

BRAHMAVAIVARTA PURANA

The Brahmavaivarta Purana is one of the eighteen major Puranas of Hinduism, believed to have originated in the 10th or 11th century AD. It is dedicated to Lord Krishna and focuses on his stories, teachings, and worship.

The Purana is divided into four parts: Brahma Khanda, Prakriti Khanda, Ganapati Khanda, and Krishna Janma Khanda. The Brahma Khanda deals with creation and cosmology, while the Prakriti Khanda focuses on the Goddess Devi. The Ganapati Khanda is dedicated to Lord Ganesha, and the Krishna Janma Khanda is the most important section, covering the life and teachings of Lord Krishna.

The Krishna Janma Khanda begins with the creation of the universe and narrates the birth and childhood of Lord Krishna. It describes his battles with demons, his relationships with the gopis, and his divine teachings. The Purana also includes teachings on spiritual practices such as yoga, meditation, and devotion to Lord Krishna.

A significant aspect of the Brahmavaivarta Purana is its emphasis on the worship of Lord Krishna. It outlines rituals, chanting of his name, recitation of his stories, and offerings. Devotion to Krishna is highlighted as the path to liberation from the cycle of birth and death.

Overall, the Brahmavaivarta Purana is a revered text in Hinduism dedicated to Lord Krishna. It provides inspiration and guidance to devotees and holds a significant place in the Hindu literary and spiritual tradition.

ॐॐॐ

THIRTY-FIVE
LINGA PURANA

The Linga Purana is one of the 18 Mahapuranas of Hinduism, believed to have been composed in the 7th or 8th century CE. It is dedicated to the worship of Lord Shiva in his form as the linga, symbolizing divine energy.

Considered an important Shaivite scripture, the Linga Purana is divided into two parts. The first part explains the creation of the universe, yugas (ages), and the cycle of birth and death. It emphasizes devotion and various forms of yoga for spiritual liberation.

The second part focuses on the worship of Lord Shiva in his linga form. It provides detailed instructions for performing puja and rituals for the linga, along with the associated benefits and blessings. The Purana also covers different forms of Shiva and their associated stories.

The Shiva Gita, a notable section of the Linga Purana, contains Lord Shiva's teachings to Parvati. It discusses the nature of the self, the importance of spiritual practice, and the path to liberation.

The Linga Purana contains numerous stories and legends related to Lord Shiva, including his marriage to Parvati, the tale of the demon Jalandhara, and the churning of the ocean of milk. It also emphasizes the significance of holy places and the merits of pilgrimage.

The Linga Purana has had a significant influence on Shaivism, particularly in South India. Many rituals and practices associated with the worship of Lord Shiva in his linga form trace their origins to this scripture.

In conclusion, the Linga Purana is an important Shaivite scripture providing profound knowledge on the universe and the worship of Lord Shiva. Its teachings continue to inspire and guide devotees of Lord Shiva today.

ॐॐॐ

THIRTY-SIX
VARAHA PURANA

The Varaha Purana is one of the eighteen Mahapuranas, sacred texts of Hinduism. It is believed to have been composed in Sanskrit by the sage Romaharshana, also known as Ugrashrava. The Purana is named after Varaha, the boar-headed avatar of Lord Vishnu, who is the main deity revered in this text.

With ten thousand verses, the Varaha Purana is divided into three parts or khandas. The first part, Prakriya Kanda, delves into cosmology, creation, and the nature of the universe. The second part, Anushanga Kanda, focuses on rituals and worship. The third and final part, Upasana Kanda, discusses the significance of devotion and the worship of various deities.

The Prakriya Kanda begins with a conversation between the sage Narada and the god Brahma. It describes the creation of the universe, the roles of Brahma, Vishnu, and Shiva in its formation, and the diverse forms within the universe. The Purana also provides detailed descriptions of the various realms or lokas that are believed to exist.

The Anushanga Kanda contains instructions for performing rituals and worshiping different deities. It underscores the importance of virtuous actions and the consequences of sinful deeds. The Purana also includes descriptions of holy places and the benefits of visiting them.

The Upasana Kanda is dedicated to the worship of various deities, such as Lord Vishnu and his avatars, Lord Shiva, and the divine mother, Devi. It describes the advantages of worshiping each deity and provides detailed instructions for their worship.

ᐅᐅᐅ

THIRTY-SEVEN
SKANDA PURANA

The Skanda Purana is one of the 18 Mahapuranas of Hinduism, believed to have been composed in Sanskrit during the medieval period. It is considered the largest Mahapurana, comprising 81,000 verses and 230 chapters. Dedicated to the worship of Lord Skanda, also known as Kartikeya or Murugan, the son of Lord Shiva and Parvati, the Skanda Purana is divided into seven books or Khandas, each focusing on a different theme.

The first book, Mahatmya Khanda, describes the greatness of Lord Skanda and his various manifestations. The second book, Vaishnava Khanda, describes the forms of Lord Vishnu and his avatars. The third book, Brahma Khanda, provides information about the creation of the universe and the various gods and goddesses. The fourth book, Kashi Khanda, is dedicated to the city of Kashi (Varanasi) and its significance. The fifth book, Avantya Khanda, describes the holy places in and around the Avanti region (present-day Ujjain). The sixth book, Nagara Khanda, explores the rituals and practices of Shaivism, including the worship of Lord Shiva. The seventh book, Prabhasa Khanda, describes the holy places associated with Lord Shiva and Lord Vishnu.

The Skanda Purana also contains numerous stories and legends from Hindu mythology. One prominent story is the birth of Lord

Skanda, also known as the Kartikeya Mahatmya. It recounts how the gods sought Lord Shiva's help to defeat the demons, and Lord Shiva manifested as six sparks of fire. The sparks were nurtured by the Krittika sisters and merged to form Lord Skanda, who subsequently defeated the demons and restored peace.

Another famous story is the churning of the ocean, known as the Samudra Manthan. It narrates how the gods and demons churned the ocean to obtain the nectar of immortality. During the process, various objects emerged, including the wish-fulfilling cow, the goddess of wealth, and deadly poison. Lord Shiva consumed the poison to save the world, resulting in his throat turning blue and earning him the name Neelakantha.

The Skanda Purana emphasizes the importance of pilgrimage and the worship of Lord Skanda. It describes holy places associated with Lord Skanda, including the six abodes (Arupadaiveedu) in Tamil Nadu, where Lord Murugan is worshipped. The Purana also details various rituals and practices associated with the worship of Lord Skanda, such as the Skanda Shasti festival.

In conclusion, the Skanda Purana holds significance as an important scripture in Hinduism, focusing on the worship of Lord Skanda and the value of pilgrimage. It features numerous stories and legends from Hindu mythology, providing insights into the beliefs and practices of Hindu tradition.

ᗰᗰᗰ

THIRTY-EIGHT
VAMANA PURANA

The Vamana Purana is one of the eighteen major Puranas in Hinduism, dedicated to the worship of Lord Vishnu. It was composed in Sanskrit between the 11th and 14th centuries CE. The Purana primarily focuses on the story of Vamana, the fifth incarnation of Lord Vishnu, who took the form of a dwarf Brahmin to defeat the demon king Bali.

The Vamana Purana is divided into two parts. The first part, Purva-khanda, contains 54 chapters and covers the creation of the universe, stories of gods and sages, and genealogy of the Solar and Lunar dynasties. The second part, Uttara-khanda, consists of 45 chapters and focuses on the life and exploits of Lord Vamana.

The Purva-khanda describes the creation of the universe, incarnations of Lord Vishnu, and the famous story of the churning of the ocean of milk. The Uttara-khanda narrates the story of Vamana, where he approaches the demon king Bali as a dwarf Brahmin, requests three paces of land, and then reveals his true form to defeat Bali.

The Vamana Purana also provides detailed descriptions of rituals and festivals dedicated to Lord Vishnu, such as Ekadashi fast and Vamana Dwadashi. It includes stories of other Hindu deities like

Shiva, Brahma, Saraswati, and Lakshmi. The Purana also mentions holy places and pilgrimage sites associated with Lord Vishnu.

Overall, the Vamana Purana is an important scripture for Lord Vishnu's devotees, offering insights into Hindu mythology, rituals, and traditions. It serves as a valuable resource for scholars and researchers studying Hinduism.

ᗎᗎᗎ

THIRTY-NINE
KURMA PURANA

The Kurma Purana is one of the eighteen major Puranas in Hinduism, dedicated to Lord Vishnu's Kurma avatar (tortoise incarnation). Composed in the medieval period, it contains six chapters with approximately 17,000 verses.

The first chapter narrates the story of the Kurma avatar, where Lord Vishnu took the form of a tortoise to help the gods obtain the nectar of immortality during their battle with demons.

The second chapter discusses the rituals and worship associated with the Kurma avatar, including fasting, meditation, and mantra recitation.

The third chapter highlights the blessings gained by studying and reciting the Kurma Purana, such as wealth, good health, and spiritual enlightenment.

The fourth chapter contains stories of notable kings and sages, including their exploits and teachings.

The fifth chapter focuses on holy places and pilgrimage sites related to the Kurma avatar, emphasizing their significance and benefits.

The final chapter delves into the dissolution and creation of the universe, with Lord Vishnu's role in the process.

Overall, the Kurma Purana serves as an important text in Hindu mythology, recounting the story of Lord Vishnu's Kurma avatar and offering guidance on associated rituals, while also providing teachings on spirituality, morality, and the nature of the universe.

ꗍꗍꗍ

FORTY
MATSYA PURANA

The Matsya Purana is one of the eighteen Mahapuranas of Hinduism, believed to have been composed in the 6th century CE. It consists of 291 chapters and is divided into two parts.

The first part focuses on the creation of the world, the origin of deities, and the genealogy of kings. It begins with the story of Lord Vishnu's Matsya avatar, where he saves the world from a great flood. The Purana then describes the origins of various deities and traces the lineage of kings.

The second part delves into religious rituals and practices. It provides detailed descriptions of yagnas, puja, and other ceremonies. It emphasizes the importance of righteousness, actions, and liberation.

The Matsya Purana highlights the worship of Lord Vishnu and describes his different avatars, such as Matsya, Kurma, Varaha, and Vamana. It emphasizes devotion and various paths to attain liberation.

The Purana contains stories of Lord Vishnu's avatars, including the rescue of the earth by Varaha and the tricking of demon king Bali by Vamana.

Overall, the Matsya Purana is a significant scripture in Hinduism, offering insights into religious practices and the worship of Lord Vishnu. Its detailed descriptions of rituals make it valuable for scholars and practitioners of Hinduism.

ᐁᐁᐁ

FORTY-ONE
GARUDA PURANA

The Garuda Purana is a significant Hindu Purana dedicated to Lord Vishnu's mount, Garuda. It consists of three parts or kandas, with the second kanda being the most renowned. This section focuses on death and the afterlife, as Lord Vishnu supposedly narrates the soul's journey after death to Garuda.

According to the Garuda Purana, after death, the soul undergoes judgment in Yamaloka, governed by the god of death, Yama. The soul is then assigned to one of the 28 hells or 21 heavens based on its actions during life. Sinners face severe punishments in the hells, including excruciating pain and suffering, while virtuous individuals are rewarded with pleasurable experiences in the heavens.

Beyond its descriptions of the afterlife, the Garuda Purana covers various other subjects. It provides insights into astrology, including calculations and predictions. It also discusses medicinal plants and their properties, along with exploring concepts of self, the universe, and the purpose of human existence.

Overall, the Garuda Purana serves as a comprehensive text encompassing a wide array of topics. Its detailed accounts of the afterlife and the consequences of actions have significantly influenced Hindu beliefs and practices. Additionally, it contributes to the understanding of astrology, medicine, and philosophy within the Hindu tradition.

ॐॐॐ

FORTY-TWO

BRAHMANDA PURANA

The Brahmānda Purāṇa, one of the eighteen Mahapuranas, is a significant part of Brahmic literature. It is known as the "Cosmic Purana" and explores the creation and evolution of the universe. Divided into two parts, the Pūrvabhāga and the Uttarabhāga, it consists of approximately 12,000 verses.

The Pūrvabhāga covers the creation of the universe, the genealogy of gods and demons, incarnations of Lord Vishnu, and the geography of the universe. It details the formation of celestial bodies, the origin of yugas, and the lineage of deities. It also narrates stories of Lord Vishnu's avatars and includes information on realms and their inhabitants.

The Uttarabhāga focuses on topics such as dharma and moksha. It discusses the importance of yoga, meditation, charity, and compassion in attaining liberation. Notably, it contains the Brahma Gita, a conversation between Lord Brahmā and Lord Vishnu about the ultimate reality and its attainment.

The Brahmānda Purāṇa also contains numerous stories and legends of gods, goddesses, and sages, including Lord Shiva, Goddess

Parvati, and Narada. It explains rituals, yajnas, the significance of holy places, and various festivals.

Overall, the Brahmānda Purāṇa provides a comprehensive understanding of Hindu cosmology, mythology, and philosophy. It is a valuable source for exploring the intricacies of Hinduism.

ᐁᐁᐁ

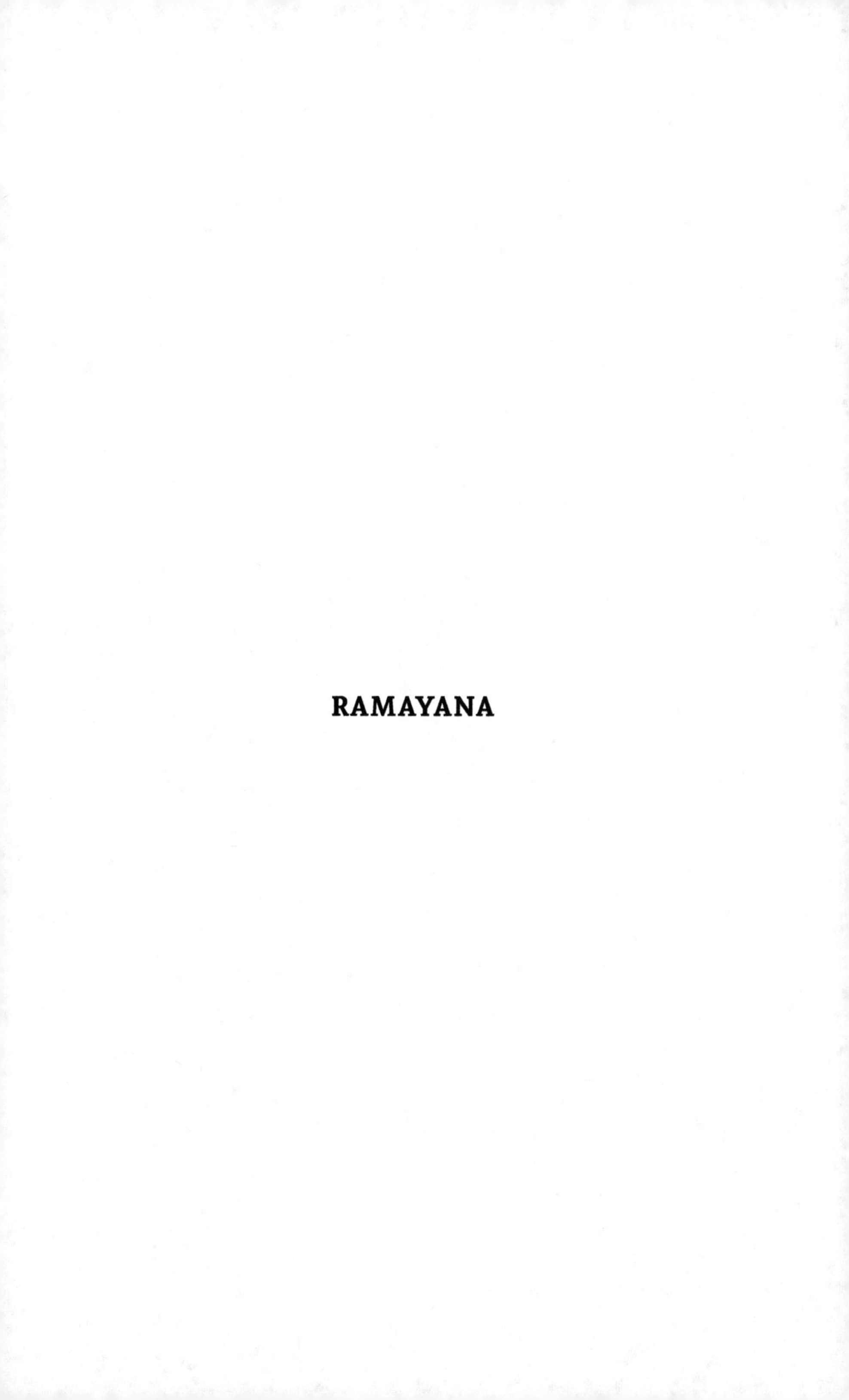

RAMAYANA

FORTY-THREE
INTRODUCTION TO RAMAYANA

The Ramayana is one of the two great Hindu epics, the other being the Mahabharata. It tells the story of Lord Rama, the seventh avatar of Lord Vishnu, and his journey from exile to the rescue of his wife Sita from the demon king Ravana.

The story is set in ancient India and revolves around the kingdom of Ayodhya. King Dasharatha, the ruler of Ayodhya, has four sons, the eldest being Rama. Rama is loved by all for his virtue, bravery, and kind-heartedness. However, Dasharatha is tricked into exiling Rama for 14 years due to a promise he had made to one of his wives, Kaikeyi.

Rama, accompanied by his wife Sita and his loyal brother Lakshmana, goes into exile and wanders through the forests. Meanwhile, Ravana, the demon king of Lanka, hears of Sita's beauty and kidnaps her, taking her back to Lanka. Rama and Lakshmana, along with the help of Hanuman and his monkey army, journey to Lanka to rescue Sita and defeat Ravana.

The Ramayana is not just a story of a hero's journey but also a tale of love, sacrifice, and devotion. It teaches the values of righteousness, dharma, and selflessness. The story is filled with characters such as Rama, Sita, Lakshmana, Hanuman, and Ravana who have become iconic in Indian mythology and culture.

The Ramayana is divided into seven books or Kandas. The first book is called Bala Kanda and tells the story of Rama's birth and childhood. The second book, Ayodhya Kanda, describes Rama's exile and the events that led up to it. The third book, Aranya Kanda, tells the story of Rama's time in the forest and his encounter with Surpanakha, Ravana's sister. The fourth book, Kishkindha Kanda, narrates the story of Rama's alliance with Hanuman and the monkey army. The fifth book, Sundara Kanda, describes Hanuman's journey to Lanka to search for Sita. The sixth book, Yuddha Kanda, is the story of the battle between Rama and Ravana. The seventh book, Uttara Kanda, tells the story of Rama's return to Ayodhya and his coronation as king.

The Ramayana has been retold in various forms over the centuries, including poetry, dance, and theater. It has also been adapted into various languages and has had a significant impact on Indian culture and society. The story of Rama and his journey continues to inspire people to this day, emphasizing the importance of righteousness, love, and devotion in one's life.

ॐॐॐ

FORTY-FOUR
BALA KANDA

The Ramayana is one of the two major epics of Hinduism, alongside the Mahabharata. It tells the story of the prince Rama, who is sent into exile by his father King Dasharatha, and his subsequent quest to rescue his wife Sita from the demon king Ravana. The Ramayana is divided into seven kandas or books, the first of which is the Bala Kanda.

The Bala Kanda opens with a description of the great sage Valmiki, who is approached by the divine sage Narada. Narada asks Valmiki whether he knows of any perfect human being on earth, and Valmiki replies that he does not. Narada then tells Valmiki the story of Rama, and how he is the perfect human being. Inspired by the story, Valmiki composes the Ramayana.

The Bala Kanda also describes the birth and childhood of Rama. Rama is the eldest son of King Dasharatha of Ayodhya, and is known for his piety and courage. He is also greatly loved by his three younger brothers, Bharata, Lakshmana, and Shatrughna. The book describes Rama's education and training in various arts and sciences, and his marriage to Sita.

The Bala Kanda also introduces the character of Ravana, the demon king of Lanka. Ravana is depicted as a powerful and fearsome figure, with ten heads and twenty arms. He is a devout worshipper of Lord Shiva, and is feared by gods and humans alike. Ravana is introduced as a villain early on in the story, and his desire for Sita sets in motion the events that will lead to the epic battle between Rama and Ravana.

The Bala Kanda also contains several other notable episodes, such as the story of how the sage Vishvamitra takes Rama and Lakshmana with him to protect his sacrifice from demon attacks, and the story of how the demoness Tataka is slain by Rama and Lakshmana.

Overall, the Bala Kanda sets the stage for the epic tale of the Ramayana, introducing the key characters and themes of the story. It establishes Rama as a paragon of virtue and righteousness, and sets up the conflict between him and Ravana. The Bala Kanda is a significant part of Hindu mythology and continues to be an important cultural touchstone in India and other parts of the world.

ᐅᐅᐅ

FORTY-FIVE
AYODHYA KANDA

The Ayodhya Kanda is the second book of the Ramayana, one of the two great Indian epic poems. It is composed of 119 chapters and tells the story of the events leading up to the exile of Lord Rama, the seventh avatar of Lord Vishnu, and his wife Sita, from the kingdom of Ayodhya. The Ayodhya Kanda is considered to be one of the most important sections of the Ramayana as it sets the stage for the epic journey that follows.

The Ayodhya Kanda begins with the events that lead up to the birth of Lord Rama. The King of Ayodhya, Dasaratha, has three wives but no children. He decides to perform a yajna to please the gods and seek their blessings for a child. The gods are pleased with his devotion and grant him four sons, Rama, Bharata, Lakshmana, and Shatrughna. Lord Rama is the eldest and is loved by all.

As Rama grows up, he becomes an expert in archery and other skills. He falls in love with Sita, the daughter of King Janaka of Mithila, and asks for her hand in marriage. King Janaka is pleased with Rama and agrees to the marriage. However, King Dasaratha soon faces a dilemma when Kaikeyi, his third wife, demands that her son Bharata be crowned king instead of Rama.

Kaikeyi has saved Dasaratha's life in the past, and he owes her two boons. She demands that Rama be exiled for fourteen years and that Bharata be made the king. Dasaratha is heartbroken but is duty-bound to fulfill his promise to Kaikeyi. Rama, Sita, and Lakshmana leave Ayodhya and head towards the forest.

The Ayodhya Kanda tells the story of the preparations for Rama's exile and his departure from Ayodhya. The people of Ayodhya are devastated by Rama's departure, and there is widespread mourning throughout the kingdom. The grief of Dasaratha is particularly poignant, and he dies soon after Rama's departure.

The Ayodhya Kanda also tells the story of the journey of Rama, Sita, and Lakshmana through the forests of India. They encounter many challenges along the way, including demons and other supernatural beings. Rama and Lakshmana fight bravely against these adversaries, and they are aided by various sages and hermits.

The Ayodhya Kanda also introduces many of the key characters of the Ramayana, including Hanuman, the monkey god, and his army of monkeys, who become important allies of Rama in his battle against Ravana, the demon king of Lanka.

The Ayodhya Kanda ends with Rama, Sita, and Lakshmana settling in the forest of Panchavati, where they live for many years. The events of the Ayodhya Kanda set the stage for the rest of the Ramayana, which tells the story of Rama's battle against Ravana and his eventual return to Ayodhya, where he is crowned king.

In conclusion, the Ayodhya Kanda of the Ramayana is an important section of the epic poem, as it sets the stage for the rest of the story. It introduces many of the key characters and themes of the Ramayana and tells the story of the events that lead up to Rama's exile from Ayodhya. The Ayodhya Kanda is a rich and complex narrative that is full of adventure, tragedy, and heroism.

ॐॐॐ

FORTY-SIX
ARANYA KANDA

The Aranya Kanda is the third book of the Ramayana, one of the most significant and ancient epics of Hindu literature. It is also known as the "Forest Book" and is composed of 75 chapters that tell the story of Rama's exile into the forest along with his wife Sita and his brother Lakshmana. In this book, the trio experiences a series of adventures, encounters various sages, and battles with powerful demons.

The Aranya Kanda begins with Rama, Sita, and Lakshmana living in the forest of Chitrakuta after leaving Ayodhya. They encounter a rakshasa named Viradha, who abducts Sita but is eventually defeated by Rama. The trio then meets the sage Sharabhanga, who advises them to move deeper into the forest to avoid further danger.

As they travel further into the forest, they come across the sages Sarabhanga, Sutikshna, and Agastya, who offer them advice and guidance. They also meet the demon Kabandha, who is initially hostile but is ultimately revealed to be a powerful being cursed by a Brahmin. Rama and Lakshmana help Kabandha attain salvation, and he advises them to seek out the monkey king Sugriva.

The brothers then meet Hanuman, a monkey prince and a devotee of Rama, who helps them form an alliance with Sugriva. Sugriva agrees to help Rama find Sita in exchange for his assistance in defeating Sugriva's brother Vali, who had wronged him.

Rama and Sugriva then make a plan to defeat Vali, and Rama eventually kills him with an arrow. Sugriva becomes the king of the monkeys and sends his army to search for Sita. They soon discover that she has been taken by the demon king Ravana and is being held captive in Lanka.

The Aranya Kanda ends with Rama and his allies planning a campaign to rescue Sita from Ravana's clutches. Overall, the book is significant as it sets the stage for the rest of the Ramayana, introducing important characters, themes, and conflicts that are central to the epic's narrative. The Aranya Kanda emphasizes the importance of loyalty, devotion, and the pursuit of righteousness, even in the face of adversity.

ᗡᗡᗡ

FORTY-SEVEN
KISHKINDA KANDA

The Kishkindha Kanda is the fourth book of the epic Hindu poem, the Ramayana. It is named after the kingdom of Kishkindha, which is ruled by the monkey king Sugriva and his ministers. This Kanda covers the period of Ram's search for his wife Sita, who has been kidnapped by the demon king Ravana, and the assistance he receives from the monkey army led by Sugriva and Hanuman.

The Kanda begins with Lord Rama and Lakshmana meeting Hanuman and Sugriva, who had been banished from his kingdom by his brother Vali. Sugriva promises to help Rama in his search for Sita, in return for Rama's promise to help him defeat Vali and regain his kingdom. Rama and Sugriva then take an oath of friendship, sealing it with a ring that bears Rama's name.

Sugriva sends his monkey army to search for Sita, and after several false leads, Hanuman finds her imprisoned in the island kingdom of Lanka. Hanuman reports his findings to Rama and Sugriva, and they plan an attack on Ravana's kingdom to rescue Sita. The Kanda also includes the famous episode of Hanuman crossing the ocean to Lanka, where he meets Sita, gives her Rama's ring, and destroys parts of Lanka with his strength.

In the meantime, Vali, Sugriva's brother, learns of his alliance with

Rama and accuses him of treachery. Rama intervenes and kills Vali with an arrow, fulfilling his promise to Sugriva. Sugriva then becomes the king of Kishkindha, with Hanuman as his trusted adviser.

The Kanda ends with Rama and his army setting out for Lanka to rescue Sita, with the support of the monkey army. This Kanda highlights the importance of loyalty and friendship, as well as the power of devotion and the importance of perseverance in the face of adversity.

In addition to the events described in the Kanda, it also includes philosophical discussions on dharma, karma, and the nature of the soul. It also describes the culture and customs of the monkey kingdom, as well as the geography of India during that time.

Overall, the Kishkindha Kanda is a significant part of the Ramayana, showcasing the importance of trust, loyalty, and perseverance. It is also a reminder of the power of faith and devotion in overcoming obstacles and achieving one's goals.

ῥῥῥ

FORTY-EIGHT
SUNDARA KANDA

The Sundara Kanda is the fifth book of the Hindu epic Ramayana. It is considered to be one of the most important and widely-read sections of the Ramayana, as it contains the story of Hanuman, the monkey god and his search for Sita, the wife of Lord Rama. The Sundara Kanda is named after the beauty and purity of Hanuman's devotion to Rama, which is said to be the central theme of this book.

The Sundara Kanda is a story of courage, determination, and unwavering devotion. It begins with the arrival of Hanuman in Lanka, the kingdom of the demon king Ravana. Hanuman is on a mission to find Sita, who has been abducted by Ravana and is being held captive in his palace. Hanuman's journey to Lanka is described in great detail, and the text includes many vivid descriptions of the landscapes and natural features of the region.

Once in Lanka, Hanuman begins his search for Sita. He encounters many obstacles and faces numerous challenges along the way, but he never gives up. He uses his strength and cunning to outwit his enemies and overcome the difficulties that he encounters. Along the way, he meets many interesting characters, including Jambavan, the wise bear; Sampati, the vulture; and Vibhishana, Ravana's younger brother, who helps Hanuman in his quest.

The most famous scene in the Sundara Kanda is Hanuman's meeting with Sita in the Ashoka grove. Sita is overjoyed to see Hanuman, and he reassures her that Rama will come to rescue her soon. Hanuman then embarks on a rampage in Lanka, destroying much of Ravana's army and causing chaos in the city. He returns to Rama with the news of Sita's whereabouts, and this sets the stage for the final battle between Rama and Ravana.

The Sundara Kanda is considered to be a powerful spiritual text that contains many important lessons for the reader. It teaches the importance of unwavering devotion and the power of faith, as Hanuman never loses hope or faith in his mission to find Sita. It also teaches the importance of courage and determination in the face of adversity, as Hanuman faces many challenges and obstacles on his journey. Finally, it teaches the importance of loyalty and friendship, as Hanuman forms strong bonds with many of the characters he meets along the way.

In addition to its spiritual significance, the Sundara Kanda is also considered to be a literary masterpiece. It is written in beautiful Sanskrit verse, and contains many vivid and poetic descriptions of the natural world. The characters are complex and well-developed, and the plot is full of twists and turns that keep the reader engaged from beginning to end.

Overall, the Sundara Kanda is an important and inspiring part of the Ramayana. It contains a powerful message of devotion, courage, and friendship, and its beautiful language and vivid descriptions make it a joy to read. It continues to be widely read and studied by scholars and spiritual seekers around the world, and its timeless message of love and devotion continues to inspire and uplift readers of all ages.

ᕤᕤᕤ

FORTY-NINE

YUDDHA KAND (LANKA KAND)

The Yuddha Kanda, also known as the Book of War, is the sixth and final book of the ancient Indian epic, the Ramayana. This book chronicles the war between Lord Rama and Ravana, the demon king of Lanka, and how Rama ultimately emerged victorious.

The Yuddha Kanda begins with Ravana's brother, Vibhishana, defecting to Rama's side and offering strategic advice on how to defeat Ravana's army. Rama then builds a bridge across the ocean to Lanka with the help of the Vanara army led by Hanuman. The battle between Rama's army and Ravana's army is fierce and brutal, with both sides displaying great courage and skill.

The highlight of the Yuddha Kanda is the battle between Rama and Ravana. The two warriors engage in a fierce duel, with each displaying incredible strength and skill. Ravana is a formidable opponent, and he is able to withstand many of Rama's attacks. However, Rama eventually gains the upper hand and is able to strike Ravana with a fatal blow.

Before dying, Ravana expresses his admiration for Rama's bravery and nobility, and advises him to rule with wisdom and compassion.

Rama then returns to Ayodhya with Sita and is welcomed back as a hero. The Ramayana ends with Rama's coronation as the king of Ayodhya.

The Yuddha Kanda is considered to be one of the most important parts of the Ramayana, as it symbolizes the triumph of good over evil. The book is also a testament to the power of faith and devotion, as Rama and his allies are able to overcome seemingly insurmountable odds through their unwavering belief in righteousness and justice.

The Yuddha Kanda also contains important teachings on leadership and governance. Rama is portrayed as an ideal king who rules with justice, compassion, and wisdom. His victory over Ravana is not just a triumph of physical strength, but also a triumph of moral and ethical values.

Overall, the Yuddha Kanda is a powerful and inspiring story that has captivated audiences for centuries. Its message of hope, faith, and righteousness continues to resonate with people of all ages and backgrounds.

ᛩᛩᛩ

FIFTY
UTTARA KANDA

The Uttara Kanda is the seventh and final section of the Hindu epic Ramayana. It is also known as the Uttararamayana or the Last Book of Ramayana. This section is believed to have been composed by different authors at different times and added to the original Ramayana.

The Uttara Kanda starts with the coronation of Rama as the king of Ayodhya and his reign of righteousness and prosperity. However, the section also contains some controversial and objectionable content, including the banishment of Sita, the birth of Lava and Kusha, and the death of Rama.

The first chapter of the Uttara Kanda describes Rama's peaceful rule as the king of Ayodhya for many years. The people of Ayodhya were happy and prosperous under his wise and just rule. Rama's brothers, Bharata, Lakshmana, and Shatrughna, also ruled their respective kingdoms with the same values.

In the second chapter, Rama overhears a conversation between a washerman and his wife, where the washerman refuses to take his wife back because she had spent time in Ravana's captivity. Rama realizes that some people in his kingdom still doubt Sita's chastity, and so he decides to banish her to the forest.

The third chapter describes Sita's banishment and her decision to go to the hermitage of Valmiki. There, she gives birth to twin sons, Lava and Kusha, who are raised by Valmiki and trained in the art of warfare and music.

The fourth chapter describes how Rama discovers the existence of his sons and goes to meet them in the forest. However, he does not recognize them and engages in a battle with them, which is eventually resolved when Valmiki reveals their true identity.

The fifth chapter describes how Lava and Kusha return to Ayodhya and perform the Ramayana in front of Rama and his court. Rama is pleased with their performance and decides to crown them as his successors.

The sixth chapter describes the battle between Rama and his sons against the invading army of the demon king, Shambuka. Rama is killed in this battle, and his soul returns to Vaikuntha, the abode of Lord Vishnu.

The final chapter of the Uttara Kanda describes the mourning of Rama's family and followers, and how Sita decides to end her life by entering the fire. However, she is saved by Agni, the god of fire, and returns to the earth to live a peaceful life in the hermitage of Valmiki.

Despite its controversial content, the Uttara Kanda is still considered an important part of the Ramayana. It provides a glimpse into the challenges faced by Rama and Sita in their reign and their unwavering commitment to righteousness and justice.

ܘܘܘ

MAHABHARATA

FIFTY-ONE
MAHABHARATAM

The Mahabharata is one of the two major Sanskrit epics of ancient India, the other being the Ramayana. It is an epic poem consisting of over 100,000 verses divided into 18 books. The story of the Mahabharata revolves around the two branches of a royal family, the Kauravas and the Pandavas, and their struggle for the throne of Hastinapur. The epic is a rich source of Indian mythology, philosophy, and spirituality, and it continues to be an important part of the Hindu tradition to this day.

The Mahabharata is believed to have been composed over a period of several centuries, from around 400 BCE to 400 CE. The authorship of the epic is traditionally attributed to the sage Vyasa, although the actual composition may have been the work of many different authors and scribes over the centuries.

The Mahabharata is divided into 18 books or parvas, each of which contains a different part of the story. The first book, the Adi Parva, describes the origins of the epic and the birth of the Kuru and Pandava princes. The following books, the Sabha Parva and the Vana Parva, describe the events leading up to the great war between the Kauravas and the Pandavas, including the famous episode of Draupadi's humiliation in the court of the Kuru king.

The central book of the Mahabharata is the Bhagavad Gita, which forms part of the sixth book, the Bhisma Parva. The Bhagavad Gita is a dialogue between the Pandava prince Arjuna and the god Krishna, who teaches Arjuna about the nature of the self, the universe, and the ultimate goal of human life.

The war between the Kauravas and the Pandavas is the subject of the next six books, the Drona Parva, the Karna Parva, the Shalya Parva, the Sauptika Parva, the Stri Parva, and the Shanti Parva. The final book, the Ashvamedhika Parva, describes the aftermath of the war and the eventual death of the Pandavas.

The Mahabharata is not only a great work of literature, but also an important source of Hindu mythology and philosophy. The epic contains many stories and teachings that are still revered by Hindus today, such as the story of the god Vishnu's incarnation as Krishna, and the teachings of the Bhagavad Gita.

One of the central themes of the Mahabharata is dharma, the Hindu concept of righteousness and duty. The story of the Kauravas and the Pandavas is a powerful illustration of the importance of following dharma, even in the face of great adversity.

Another important theme of the Mahabharata is karma, the Hindu concept of the law of cause and effect. The epic portrays the consequences of actions, both good and bad, and emphasizes the importance of living a life of righteousness and virtue.

The Mahabharata is also an important source of inspiration for the arts and culture of India. The epic has inspired countless works of literature, music, and theater, and its characters and stories continue to be beloved by people of all ages.

In conclusion, the Mahabharata is a masterpiece of Indian literature and a vital part of the Hindu tradition. Its timeless teachings and profound insights into the human condition continue to resonate with people around the world, making it one of the greatest works of literature in human history.

ϷϷϷ

FIFTY-TWO
ADI PARVAM

The Adi Parva, the first book of the Mahabharata, serves as the foundation for the epic. It introduces key characters and provides essential background information. The story begins with King Janamejaya seeking revenge for his father's death, and during a grand sacrifice, the sage Vaisampayana recites the Mahabharata to him and his court.

The Adi Parva delves into the creation of the world, the gods, and demons, as well as the lineage of King Bharata, after whom India is named. The narrative then centers on the conflict between two sets of cousins, the Pandavas and Kauravas, who battle for control of the kingdom of Hastinapura.

Led by Yudhishthira, the Pandavas are the rightful heirs, but the Kauravas, led by Duryodhana, refuse to yield power. The Adi Parva introduces the five Pandava brothers, their mother Kunti, and their cousin Krishna, along with other important characters.

Subplots and stories in the Adi Parva include the tales of the sage Vyasa, the author of the Mahabharata, and the sage Markandeya, who possesses immortality.

The Adi Parva culminates in the famous dice game, where the

Pandavas lose their kingdom and face thirteen years of exile. This sets the stage for the rest of the epic, depicting the events leading to the great war at Kurukshetra and its aftermath.

Overall, the Adi Parva establishes the groundwork for the Mahabharata, introducing characters and providing crucial cultural and mythological context for the epic's world.

ᐺᐺᐺ

FIFTY-THREE
SABHA PARVA

The Sabha Parva, the second book of the Mahabharata, narrates the events that transpire after the Pandavas lose their kingdom to the Kauravas in a game of dice. King Yudhishthira accepts the invitation to the game and ends up losing everything, including his kingdom and his family.

The Pandavas, exiled to the forest, embark on a pilgrimage, encountering sages and overcoming demons along the way. Meanwhile, the Kauravas revel in their victory, but their immoral behavior incurs the displeasure of both people and gods.

After completing their pilgrimage, the Pandavas return to Hastinapura, only to be denied their rightful share of the kingdom by the Kauravas. They choose to spend a year in the forest to fulfill a vow, receiving guidance from their mother, Kunti.

During their exile, the Pandavas engage in religious practices and gain wisdom from sages. The Kauravas, however, continue their immoral ways, losing favor with the people.

The Sabha Parva concludes with the Pandavas' return to Hastinapura, where they are once again denied their rightful share, setting the stage for the events leading to the great war between the

Pandavas and the Kauravas.

In summary, the Sabha Parva portrays the Pandavas' journey through exile, encounters with sages and demons, and their subsequent return, while highlighting the Kauravas' moral decline. It sets the stage for the unfolding events that culminate in the epic war.

ᗏᗏᗏ

FIFTY-FOUR

VANA PARVA OR ARANYA PARVA

The Vana Parva, the third book of the Mahabharata, recounts the twelve-year exile of the Pandavas in the forest. It begins with their departure from the kingdom and follows their encounters with sages, demons, and various challenges during their stay.

The Pandavas meet renowned sages like Markandeya, Narada, and Vyasa, who impart profound wisdom on subjects such as righteousness, action, and liberation. They learn about ascetic practices and engage in philosophical discussions.

The Vana Parva provides vivid descriptions of the forest's flora and fauna, offering a rich depiction of the natural environment. It includes captivating stories like the romantic tale of Nala and Damayanti, as well as the rejuvenation of the sage Chyavana and the love story of Hidimba and Bhima.

Sage Markandeya narrates the story of King Harishchandra, emphasizing the importance of truth and sacrifice in upholding dharma. The book concludes with the Pandavas disguising themselves and entering the kingdom of King Virata, setting the stage for the events of the next book.

Overall, the Vana Parva delves into spiritual practices, ethical principles, and moral dilemmas. It offers a treasure trove of mythology, folklore, and timeless lessons that continue to inspire readers and thinkers.

FIFTY-FIVE
VIRATA PARVA

The Virata Parva is the fourth book of the Mahabharata, which narrates the Pandavas' year of exile in the kingdom of Virata. After completing their thirteen-year exile in the forest, the Pandavas spend a year living incognito in Virata's court.

During their stay, each Pandava assumes a different identity. Yudhishthira becomes a priest, Bhima works as a cook, Arjuna serves as a eunuch, Nakula takes care of horses, and Sahadeva becomes a cowherd. Meanwhile, the Kauravas discover their whereabouts and plan an attack.

However, the Pandavas successfully defend themselves and defeat the Kauravas with the help of their allies. The Virata Parva also introduces important characters like Uttara, the prince of Virata, who later plays a significant role in the Kurukshetra war.

Additionally, the Pandavas prepare for the impending battle. Arjuna visits the gods and obtains divine weapons and guidance from Lord Indra and other deities, equipping him for the forthcoming war.

Overall, the Virata Parva sets the stage for the battle of Kurukshetra, introducing crucial characters, providing insight into the Pandavas' incognito year, and preparing them for the war. It showcases themes of exile, survival, hope, determination, and the strength of the human spirit.

ϸϸϸ

FIFTY-SIX
UDYOGA PARVA

The Udyoga Parva, the fifth book of the Mahabharata, focuses on the preparations for the inevitable war between the Pandavas and the Kauravas. It begins with a debate between Krishna and Arjuna about the need for war, and they set out to negotiate a peaceful settlement with the Kauravas.

However, the negotiations fail, and war becomes unavoidable. The Udyoga Parva describes the extensive preparations made by both sides, including the recruitment of allies and the construction of massive armies.

Within the parva, there are various sub-stories, such as the tales of Nala and Damayanti, the Yaksha's questions, and Brihaspati and Shukra. These stories serve as moral lessons and illustrate different aspects of the narrative.

One of the most significant sections of the Udyoga Parva is the Bhagavad Gita, a profound dialogue between Krishna and Arjuna on the battlefield. The Bhagavad Gita addresses profound philosophical concepts and is highly regarded as a central text in Hinduism.

Throughout the Udyoga Parva, the theme of dharma (moral duty) is emphasized. The Pandavas are depicted as upholding dharma, while the Kauravas are portrayed as disregarding it. This emphasis underscores the importance of righteous conduct and the consequences of neglecting moral principles.

In summary, the Udyoga Parva plays a pivotal role in the Mahabharata, setting the stage for the impending war and providing insights into the characters and their preparations. It highlights the significance of dharma and includes the revered Bhagavad Gita, which continues to inspire and guide individuals worldwide.

ppp

FIFTY-SEVEN
BHISHMA PARVA

The Bhishma Parva is the sixth book of the Mahabharata, an ancient Indian epic. It revolves around Bhishma, a respected warrior of the Kuru clan, who is gravely wounded in a fierce battle between the Kauravas and the Pandavas. Spanning chapters 25 to 42, it is also known as the "Book of Bhishma."

The parva begins with the continuation of the war on its twelfth day. Bhishma, the Kaurava army's commander-in-chief, unleashes havoc on the Pandava forces. However, Arjuna and Bhima gradually turn the tide in favor of the Pandavas through their remarkable skills and power.

On the thirteenth day, Bhishma takes an oath not to harm any Pandava except Arjuna, as he had vowed to protect the throne of Hastinapura for the Kuru dynasty. Despite causing immense damage to the Pandava army, Bhishma is eventually defeated by Arjuna's arrows. He lies on a bed of arrows, awaiting the opportune time to renounce his life and attain salvation.

The Bhishma Parva is notable for Bhishma's teachings to Yudhishthira, the eldest Pandava, encompassing various topics such as righteousness, politics, and morality. Bhishma imparts valuable lessons on the principles of good governance, the duties of a warrior, and the significance of truth and integrity.

The parva also includes the famous "Anusasana Parva," wherein Bhishma delivers an elaborate discourse on dharma, elucidating the duties of different castes and the virtues and vices of human nature. He emphasizes the importance of righteous conduct and warns against the pitfalls of ego and attachment.

The Bhishma Parva marks a pivotal moment in the Mahabharata, symbolizing a turning point in the Kauravas' fortunes. It is a repository of profound wisdom, underscoring the importance of walking the path of righteousness while cautioning against attachment and ego. The book's enduring legacy continues to inspire and guide people to this day, exemplifying the timeless teachings of the Mahabharata.

FIFTY-EIGHT
DRONA PARVA

The Drona Parva is the seventh book of the Mahabharata, an ancient Indian epic. It is named after Drona, a mentor to the Kuru princes. The book focuses on the events leading up to the war between the Pandavas and the Kauravas, as well as the war itself, encompassing themes of love, friendship, betrayal, and sacrifice.

The Pandavas and Kauravas seek allies for the impending war. Duryodhana, the Kaurava leader, approaches Drona for support. Drona agrees, but demands the capture of Yudhishthira, the eldest Pandava. Through a game of dice, the Pandavas lose their kingdom and are exiled to the forest.

In the forest, they encounter a sage and learn about devotion to gods. Bhima defeats a demon and marries his sister. After years of learning from sages and warriors, the Pandavas return to reclaim their throne.

Complex relationships are explored, such as Arjuna's friendship with Drona's son, Ashwatthama, who becomes their enemy during the war. Drona, torn between loyalty and duty, fights for the Kauravas.

The war is brutal, resulting in numerous casualties. The Pandavas emerge victorious but mourn their losses. Philosophical discussions on righteousness, karma, and reality arise, along with religious and mythological stories.

The Drona Parva delves into human relationships, morality, and consequences. Characters are well-developed and relatable, making it a timeless classic of Indian literature.

ᐁᐁᐁ

FIFTY-NINE
KARNA PARVA

The Karna Parva is the eighth book of the Mahabharata, an ancient Indian epic. It centers around Karna, a complex and tragic character who fights on the side of the Kauravas. The book focuses on the events leading up to Karna's death and its impact on the war between the Pandavas and the Kauravas.

Karna becomes the commander of the Kaurava army after Bhishma is wounded. Despite his remarkable skills, Karna faces discrimination due to his low social status. Throughout the war, Karna struggles with conflicting loyalties and his own identity.

Key moments include Karna's battle with Arjuna, which ends inconclusively due to divine intervention. The book explores Karna's relationships, particularly with his friend Duryodhana and his enemy Bhima.

The climax occurs when Arjuna, with an unfair advantage, kills Karna. It is revealed that Karna was the eldest Pandava, adding to the tragedy. Karna's death deeply affects the other characters, especially Arjuna.

The book also discusses themes of righteousness, karma, and reality. Characters confront the moral implications of their choices.

It includes religious and mythological stories.

The Karna Parva is a powerful and emotional section of the Mahabharata, delving into human emotions, relationships, and identity. Karna's story resonates with readers, and its themes remain relevant.

❦❦❦

SIXTY
SHALYA PARVA

The Shalya Parva is the ninth book of the Mahabharata, an ancient Indian epic. It revolves around Shalya, the commander of the Kaurava army after Karna's demise. The book primarily focuses on the events leading up to the final battle between the Pandavas and the Kauravas.

As the Pandava and Kaurava armies prepare for the ultimate confrontation, Shalya, a complex character related to both sides, plays a crucial role. He is respected for his wisdom and skills as a warrior and counselor.

The book features significant moments in Shalya's story, including his interactions with the Pandava prince Yudhishthira and the Kaurava prince Duryodhana. Shalya provides wise guidance to both, emphasizing honor and righteousness. He contemplates life, death, and the importance of integrity.

Key battles, such as the fight between Bhima and Duryodhana, unfold, leading to Duryodhana's defeat and the war's conclusion. Shalya valiantly defends his king but falls to Bhima.

The climax arrives when Shalya is slain in battle by Yudhishthira, adding to the tragedy of a respected warrior forced to fight on the wrong side. His death highlights the devastating cost of war.

The book engages in philosophical discussions on righteousness, karma, and reality, challenging characters to confront moral implications and the consequences of their choices. It incorporates religious and mythological tales, including that of Varuna and Harishchandra.

Overall, the Shalya Parva is a powerful section of the Mahabharata, exploring human emotions, relationships, and identity while contemplating the impact of actions and the nature of morality. Shalya's character evokes sympathy, and the book's themes remain impactful and relevant today.

❧❧❧

SIXTY-ONE
SAUPATIKA PARVA

Sauptika Parva, the tenth book of the Mahabharata, is also known as the "Book of the Sleeping Warriors." It focuses on the aftermath of the final battle between the Pandavas and the Kauravas.

Following their victory, the Pandavas face the heavy toll of the war. They mourn the loss of loved ones and allies. The book portrays poignant scenes of grief and mourning.

A tragic event occurs when the injured Kaurava king, Duryodhana, refuses to surrender and asks his loyal friend Ashwatthama to avenge his impending death. Together, they launch a brutal attack on the sleeping Pandavas.

The attack succeeds, resulting in the death of key warriors who were unaware and defenseless. The aftermath is marked by sorrow as the surviving Pandavas seek revenge and justice against Ashwatthama.

Religious and philosophical discussions contemplate life, death, karma, and destiny. The characters reflect on the lessons learned from the war and the significance of living with honor and integrity.

The book serves as a poignant reminder of the human cost of war, showcasing the tragic consequences that even well-intentioned warriors can bring. It emphasizes the importance of compassion, forgiveness, and reconciliation in the aftermath of conflict, urging a pursuit of a more peaceful and just world.

In conclusion, Sauptika Parva remains a profound and emotionally charged part of the Mahabharata. Its themes and stories retain relevance and impact, making it a timeless gem of Indian literature.

ppp

SIXTY-TWO
STRI PARVA

Stri Parva, the eleventh book of the Mahabharata, is also known as the "Book of the Women." It centers on the perspectives of female characters, a unique departure from the male-dominated narrative of the epic.

The book begins with the aftermath of the war, where the victorious Pandavas mourn their losses and rebuild. Grief and mourning permeate the narrative as characters grapple with the tragic consequences of the war.

The first section, "Ghoshayatra," follows the journey of widows, including Gandhari and the wives of fallen Kaurava warriors, to Hastinapura. They lament their losses, critique male characters for their role in the war, and question their leadership and protection.

The second section, "Jalapradanika," portrays Queen Sudeshna's sacrifice to uphold her husband's honor, showcasing the importance of women's virtue and self-sacrifice in traditional Indian culture.

The third section, "Saubhagyavati," narrates the story of Savitri, a devoted wife who rescues her husband from death, emphasizing the power of love and devotion in overcoming challenges.

The fourth section, "Vaivahika," revolves around the marriage of the Pandavas' daughter, Uttarā, highlighting discussions on marriage, family, inheritance, and providing insights into ancient Indian social and cultural practices.

Stri Parva is a powerful and significant part of the Mahabharata, shedding light on the roles, challenges, and perspectives of women. It urges the importance of listening to diverse voices, promoting equality, and striving for justice in society.

ᐁᐁᐁ

SIXTY-THREE
SHANTI PARVA

Shanti Parva, a significant chapter in the Mahabharata, serves as a profound treatise on dharma, the guiding principle of human conduct and ethical behavior. This lengthy chapter contains invaluable teachings on morality, ethics, and spirituality that are timeless in their relevance.

Divided into three sections with a total of 365 chapters, the Shanti Parva explores various aspects of dharma. The first section, spanning 108 chapters, emphasizes the importance of dharma, the duties of rulers, and the necessity of societal harmony and peace. The second section, comprising 92 chapters, delves into the path to liberation and the essence of the soul. The final section consists of 165 chapters, covering diverse topics such as self-control, duties of householders, the significance of charity, and the power of devotion.

Central to the Shanti Parva is the profound significance of dharma. The text underscores that dharma serves as the bedrock of human existence, providing a moral framework for ethical behavior, social equilibrium, and spiritual progress. It emphasizes that every individual bears the responsibility of upholding dharma, as the conscientious fulfillment of duties leads to happiness, prosperity, and spiritual growth.

Another key theme in the Shanti Parva pertains to the nature of the soul and the path to liberation. It elucidates that the soul is eternal and imperishable, entrapped within the cycle of birth and death due to the influence of karma. The Shanti Parva expounds upon the soul's essence, delineates various stages of spiritual development, and outlines the practices that facilitate liberation.

Moreover, the Shanti Parva features captivating stories and parables illustrating the significance of dharma and the potency of spiritual discipline. Notably, the tale of the four brothers epitomizes the four stages of human life (student, householder, forest-dweller, and renunciant) and emphasizes the fulfillment of duties in each stage, providing a blueprint for spiritual progress.

In summary, the Shanti Parva presents a profound and timeless exploration of dharma and spiritual growth. It underscores the importance of upholding dharma, nurturing virtues, and pursuing spiritual practices as the means to attain happiness, prosperity, and liberation. The Shanti Parva stands as an invaluable guide for those seeking direction on the path of dharma and spiritual evolution.

ᐅᐅᐅ

SIXTY-FOUR
ANUSHASANA PARVA

Anushasana Parva, the thirteenth book of the Mahabharata, is known as the "Book of Instructions." It is a lengthy and significant section of the epic, containing detailed teachings on ethics, morality, and spirituality. Notably, it includes the renowned Bhagavad Gita, a conversation between Krishna and Arjuna on the Kurukshetra battlefield.

The book begins with sage Vyasa instructing Yudhishthira on the duties and qualities of a just and compassionate king. Vyasa emphasizes the importance of maintaining harmonious relationships with subjects and protecting the weak. The subsequent sections feature discourses by sages and hermits, providing guidance on various aspects of life, including duties as householders, the practice of yoga and meditation, and the significance of selfless service.

The Bhagavad Gita, a key component of Anushasana Parva, unfolds as Krishna enlightens Arjuna about duty, detachment, and devotion. Krishna emphasizes the need to perform one's duties without attachment to outcomes, stressing the pursuit of duty without seeking personal gain. He imparts teachings on the nature of reality and the ultimate goal of spiritual practice, which is liberation from the cycle of birth and death.

Anushasana Parva concludes with Yudhishthira's horse sacrifice, symbolizing his sovereignty, followed by a final discourse by Vyasa on upholding dharma and the consequences of neglecting one's duties.

Overall, Anushasana Parva offers profound spiritual and philosophical insights into the nature of existence and remains an enduring source of inspiration and guidance for millions worldwide.

ﬂﬂﬂ

SIXTY-FIVE

ASHVAMEDHIKA PARVA

The Ashvamedhika Parva, the fourteenth book of the Mahabharata, is known as the "Book of the Horse Sacrifice." It narrates the elaborate ritual of the Ashvamedha, performed by ancient Indian kings to assert their power over neighboring kingdoms.

Following the victorious Kurukshetra war, Yudhishthira becomes the king and decides to perform the Ashvamedha to establish his authority. The book describes the intricate preparations and rituals involved in the sacrifice, including the selection of the horse, consecration of the sacrificial ground, and various offerings and prayers. Battles ensue as Yudhishthira's brothers and warriors defend the horse from challengers.

A significant event occurs when Arjuna's son, Babruvahana, born to Chitrangada, confronts Arjuna in battle and kills him. Arjuna is later revived with Indra's help and reunited with his family.

The Ashvamedhika Parva concludes with the successful completion of the ritual, solidifying Yudhishthira's supremacy. The book ends with Vyasa's final discourse, emphasizing the importance of upholding dharma and fulfilling one's duties.

Overall, the Ashvamedhika Parva provides a detailed account of the Ashvamedha ritual and its political and social significance. It offers insights into the complex religious practices of ancient India and showcases the enduring value of the Mahabharata as a literary and spiritual masterpiece.

ᐁᐁᐁ

SIXTY-SIX

ASHRAMAVASIKA PARVA

The Ashramavasika Parva, the fifteenth book of the Mahabharata, is known as the "Book of the Hermitage." It recounts the Pandavas' final year of exile, spent in the hermitage of sage Vyasa.

After their disguised exile in the kingdom of Virata, the Pandavas and Draupadi seek refuge in Vyasa's hermitage. The book primarily consists of stories and teachings during their stay. It includes tales like the cursed king Nriga's greed and the sage Markandeya's knowledge acquisition from Lord Brahma.

The Ashramavasika Parva features the renowned story of the Mahabharata itself, narrated by sage Vaishampayana to King Janamejaya. This narrative details the conflict between the Kuru and Pandava clans, leading to the epic battle of Kurukshetra.

Teachings on morality and spirituality are abundant, emphasizing self-control, charity, and devotion to God. Sage Vyasa imparts wisdom to the Pandavas and Draupadi, guiding them on righteous living and overcoming life's challenges.

The book mourns the death of the Pandavas' dear friend and

advisor, sage Dhaumya, who played a crucial role in their survival and victory. The Pandavas deeply grieve his loss.

The Ashramavasika Parva concludes as the Pandavas and Draupadi leave Vyasa's hermitage to reclaim their rightful place in the kingdom of Hastinapura. It underscores the significance of wisdom, morality, and spirituality in adversity, demonstrating the enduring power of faith and devotion.

ϷϷϷ

SIXTY-SEVEN
MAUSALA PARVA

The Mausala Parva, the sixteenth book of the Mahabharata, is known as the "Book of the Clubs." It depicts the aftermath of the Pandavas' victory in the Kurukshetra war against the Kauravas.

The book starts with the death of Lord Krishna, struck by a hunter's arrow named Jara. Krishna's demise marks the end of an era, causing grief and turmoil throughout the kingdom.

The Mausala Parva focuses on the aftermath of Krishna's death. It portrays a period of sorrow and chaos as the Pandavas and the people of Hastinapura struggle to cope with the loss of their beloved leader.

A significant event in the book is the outbreak of a deadly plague caused by the Mausala, clubs used as weapons in the war. The Pandavas had given the clubs to the Yadava clan, who became intoxicated and turned against each other, resulting in bloodshed. The tainted clubs led to the devastating plague.

Despite their victory, the Pandavas feel guilt and regret over the war's consequences. They attempt to reconcile with the Kauravas, offering peace gestures, but the Kauravas remain bitter and reject their gestures.

The Mausala Parva ends with the Pandavas and their allies departing from Hastinapura, embarking on their journey to the afterlife. It serves as a poignant reminder of life's impermanence and the significance of embracing the present moment. As a fitting conclusion to the Mahabharata, it continues to captivate and inspire readers.

ᢞᢞᢞ

SIXTY-EIGHT

MAHAPRASTHANIKA PARVA

The Mahaprasthanika Parva, the seventeenth book of the Mahabharata, is known as the "Book of the Great Journey." It narrates the final journey of the Pandavas towards the afterlife and their ascent to heaven.

The book begins with the Pandavas leaving their capital, Hastinapura, and embarking on a journey to the Himalayas. Accompanied by Draupadi and a dog, they receive guidance and blessings from sages and deities they encounter along the way.

As the journey progresses, one by one, the Pandavas and Draupadi fall. Yudhishthira, the eldest, remains. The god of death, Yama, appears and offers to take Yudhishthira to the afterlife. Yudhishthira requests that his loyal dog accompanies him, but Yama refuses. Yudhishthira chooses to stay with his dog and is rewarded by being granted entry into heaven.

The Mahaprasthanika Parva serves as a poignant reminder of life's impermanence and the certainty of death. It highlights the significance of loyalty and faithfulness, as shown by Yudhishthira's decision to remain with his dog.

The book also delves into profound philosophical and spiritual teachings. Yudhishthira engages in dialogues with sages and deities, seeking a deeper understanding of the universe and life's meaning. These conversations explore concepts of karma, dharma, and the afterlife, offering rich spiritual teachings that continue to inspire readers.

Beyond its spiritual and philosophical aspects, the Mahaprasthanika Parva concludes the epic tale of the Mahabharata fittingly. It brings closure to the Pandavas' journey towards self-realization and enlightenment. The book instills hope and a sense of transcendence as the Pandavas gain entry into heaven and reunite with their loved ones.

The Mahaprasthanika Parva stands as a powerful testament to the enduring strength of the human spirit and our search for purpose and meaning. It emphasizes the importance of living with intention and reminds us of our ultimate aspiration to transcend the limitations of mortal existence. It is a befitting culmination to one of the world's greatest literary epics, showcasing the lasting impact of storytelling in inspiring and uplifting humanity.

ÞÞÞ

SIXTY-NINE

SWARGAROHANA PARVA

The Svargarohana Parva, the final book of the Mahabharata, is known as the "Book of the Ascent to Heaven." It consists of two chapters and narrates the Pandavas' journey to heaven.

The parva begins with Yudhishthira lamenting the loss and violence of the war. Seeking guidance, he turns to Bhishma, who advises him on righteous rule and dharma. Bhishma shares stories of virtuous rulers and imparts wisdom on the nature of the soul.

As Bhishma speaks, he attains complete knowledge and prepares to depart. The Pandavas gather by his side, and he instructs them on achieving salvation through renunciation and atonement. Bhishma reveals the story of King Rantideva, who learned to accept suffering as a means of soul purification.

Bhishma then instructs Yudhishthira on funeral rites and peacefully passes away. The second chapter depicts the Pandavas' journey to heaven, accompanied by a dog who is revealed as the god Dharma. Yudhishthira's companions gradually fall, leaving only him and the dog.

Yudhishthira learns the dog's true identity and enters heaven, where he reunites with his brothers and Draupadi. He explores celestial realms and is crowned king of heaven. The parva concludes with the message that righteousness and devotion lead to salvation and eternal happiness.

The Svargarohana Parva serves as a profound conclusion to the Mahabharata, emphasizing the significance of moral conduct and devotion in attaining spiritual enlightenment and eternal bliss.

ᐳᐳᐳ

BHAGAVAD GITA

SEVENTY
BHAGAVAD GITA

The Bhagavad Gita is one of the most significant and revered texts in Hinduism. It is a part of the epic poem, Mahabharata, and is composed of 18 chapters. The Bhagavad Gita is often referred to as the "Song of the Lord" as it is said to be the teachings of Lord Krishna to Arjuna, a warrior prince.

The Bhagavad Gita is set in the middle of the battlefield, where the Kuru and Pandava armies are about to engage in a fierce battle. Arjuna, the Pandava prince, is filled with doubt and confusion about the righteousness of the battle, and questions Lord Krishna about it. Lord Krishna, who is also Arjuna's charioteer, provides him with answers in the form of spiritual knowledge and wisdom.

The first chapter of the Bhagavad Gita sets the stage for the rest of the text. It describes the armies assembled on both sides of the battlefield and the state of mind of Arjuna, who is filled with doubt and despair. Arjuna laments that the battle will lead to the destruction of his family and loved ones and questions the purpose of the war.

Lord Krishna responds to Arjuna's doubts by explaining the nature of the soul and the impermanence of the body. He tells Arjuna that the soul is eternal and indestructible and that death is simply the passing of the soul from one body to another. Lord Krishna also explains the concept of karma and how every action has consequences that determine one's future.

In the subsequent chapters, Lord Krishna delves deeper into the nature of the soul, the importance of devotion, and the path to spiritual enlightenment. He explains the different paths of yoga and how they can help one achieve self-realization and connect with the divine. Lord Krishna also emphasizes the importance of detachment and renunciation in achieving spiritual growth.

The Bhagavad Gita also contains famous verses that have become known worldwide. One of the most famous is the twelfth chapter, where Lord Krishna explains the qualities of a devotee and the importance of surrendering to the divine will. He also emphasizes that all paths ultimately lead to him and that devotion is the key to achieving spiritual liberation.

The eighteenth and final chapter of the Bhagavad Gita summarizes the teachings of Lord Krishna and emphasizes the importance of following one's duty without attachment to the results. It also provides a glimpse into the future of the Kuru dynasty and the fate of its various characters.

The Bhagavad Gita has been a source of inspiration for millions of people worldwide, and its teachings continue to be relevant to this day. It emphasizes the importance of spiritual growth and the path to achieving inner peace and enlightenment. The Bhagavad Gita teaches us that devotion and detachment are essential to achieving spiritual liberation and that ultimately, all paths lead to the divine.

ᛈᛈᛈ

SEVENTY-ONE
ARJUNA VISHADA YOGA

Chapter 1 of the Bhagavad Gita, titled Arjuna Vishada Yoga, lays the foundation for the teachings and principles that are to follow in the rest of the book. This chapter depicts the setting of the Mahabharata war and Arjuna's emotional and mental state upon witnessing the armies and realizing the implications of the war. The chapter is a powerful illustration of the complexities of human nature and the struggles that arise when one is faced with difficult choices.

The chapter begins with the blind king Dhritarashtra asking his advisor Sanjaya to describe the battlefield to him, as he is unable to see. Sanjaya, with the power of his divine vision, describes the armies of the Kauravas and Pandavas assembled on the battlefield, along with their respective generals.

Arjuna, one of the Pandava brothers and the protagonist of the Gita, is described as being deeply troubled and dejected upon seeing the massive armies assembled on the battlefield. He is filled with sorrow and compassion for his kinsmen and teachers who are assembled on both sides of the battle. He wonders how it is possible for him to fight against his own family members, who are his elders and teachers, and who have taught him everything he knows.

Arjuna's mental conflict is the main theme of this chapter, and it is expressed in his dialogue with Krishna, his charioteer and friend. Arjuna shares his doubts and fears with Krishna, and asks for guidance and direction. He says that he is confused and has lost his sense of duty, as he is unable to decide what is right and wrong.

Krishna, in response, reminds Arjuna of his duty as a warrior and explains the nature of the soul, the importance of detachment, and the philosophy of Karma Yoga. He emphasizes the importance of action without attachment, and encourages Arjuna to perform his duty as a warrior without being attached to the results of his actions. Krishna also explains the concept of the eternal nature of the soul and how it transcends birth and death.

The chapter ends with Arjuna, still confused and indecisive, putting down his bow and arrow and saying that he will not fight. This sets the stage for the rest of the Bhagavad Gita, where Krishna will impart his teachings and guide Arjuna towards a deeper understanding of the nature of reality, the soul, and the ultimate purpose of life.

Overall, Chapter 1 of the Bhagavad Gita sets the tone for the rest of the book, emphasizing the importance of self-realization, detachment, and action without attachment. It also portrays the struggles and conflicts of human nature, and the importance of seeking guidance and direction in times of confusion and doubt. The teachings of the Gita continue to be relevant and influential to this day, inspiring millions of people to seek spiritual growth and enlightenment.

ᡐᡐᡐ

SEVENTY-TWO
SANKHYA YOGA

Chapter 2 of the Bhagavad Gita, also known as Sankhya Yoga, is a continuation of the dialogue between Lord Krishna and Arjuna. In this chapter, Lord Krishna begins to impart the knowledge of the ultimate truth to Arjuna, and helps him understand the nature of the self, the material world, and the Supreme Being.

The chapter begins with Arjuna expressing his doubts and fears about engaging in the battle. He questions the value of fighting his own kinsmen and teachers, and wonders if it is better to renounce the world and live as an ascetic. Lord Krishna understands Arjuna's dilemma and begins to reveal the principles of Sankhya Yoga to him.

Lord Krishna tells Arjuna that his fear and doubts arise from his ignorance of the true nature of the self. He explains that the body, mind, and senses are all material in nature and temporary, and that the true self, or Atman, is eternal and indestructible. He urges Arjuna to act in accordance with his duty as a warrior, and not to be attached to the outcome of his actions.

Lord Krishna explains that the path to liberation is to perform one's duty without attachment and with a sense of detachment, offering the fruits of one's actions to the Supreme Being. He emphasizes that the performance of duty is necessary for the maintenance of the order of the world, and that renunciation is not necessary for achieving liberation.

Lord Krishna also explains the nature of the material world, which is characterized by the three modes of material nature - goodness, passion, and ignorance. He explains that attachment to material objects and desires is the cause of suffering, and that one must transcend these modes and attain the state of pure consciousness to achieve liberation.

In this chapter, Lord Krishna also explains the principles of Karma Yoga, which involves performing one's duty without attachment to the fruits of one's actions. He emphasizes that one should not be attached to the results of one's actions, but should perform them as an offering to the Supreme Being.

Lord Krishna concludes the chapter by urging Arjuna to rise above his doubts and fears, and to follow the path of wisdom and knowledge. He tells Arjuna that he is capable of achieving liberation, and that he will guide him on the path to self-realization.

In summary, Chapter 2 of the Bhagavad Gita, Sankhya Yoga, is a profound discourse on the nature of the self, the material world, and the Supreme Being. Lord Krishna teaches Arjuna the principles of Karma Yoga, and emphasizes the importance of performing one's duty without attachment. He urges Arjuna to rise above his doubts and fears, and to follow the path of wisdom and knowledge to attain liberation.

ॐॐॐ

SEVENTY-THREE
KARMA YOGA

Chapter 3 of the Bhagavad Gita is titled "Karma Yoga" or "The Yoga of Action". In this chapter, Lord Krishna instructs Arjuna on the importance of performing one's duties without attachment to the results.

Lord Krishna begins by reminding Arjuna that he has already been taught the principles of yoga in the previous chapter, and now it is time for him to learn about the yoga of action. He explains that one should perform their duties without being attached to the results, for attachment to the results of one's actions leads to disappointment, anxiety, and suffering.

Krishna further explains that everyone has a duty to perform based on their nature, and that one should not give up their duty even if it is difficult or unappealing. He states that even the wise follow the actions of their nature, and that one who abandons their duty for fear of difficulty is guilty of a great sin.

Krishna then introduces the concept of karma yoga, or the yoga of selfless action. He explains that performing one's duty without attachment to the results is the key to spiritual growth, and that one who performs their duty with a pure mind and without attachment to the results will not be bound by the consequences of their actions.

He goes on to explain that the performance of one's duty is a sacrifice to the divine, and that one who performs their duty in this way is released from the bonds of karma. Krishna also emphasizes that one should not expect any reward for their actions, but should simply do their duty for the sake of doing it.

Krishna then elaborates on the nature of action, explaining that there are three types of action: karma yoga (selfless action), akarma (inaction), and vikarma (forbidden action). He states that one should perform selfless action and avoid forbidden action, and that inaction is not an option, for even the act of not acting is an action in itself.

Krishna concludes this chapter by reiterating the importance of performing one's duty without attachment to the results, and by emphasizing that karma yoga is the path to liberation. He encourages Arjuna to rise above his attachment to the results of his actions and to focus on performing his duty with a pure mind and heart.

In summary, Chapter 3 of the Bhagavad Gita teaches the importance of performing one's duty without attachment to the results, and introduces the concept of karma yoga as the path to spiritual growth and liberation. It emphasizes the importance of performing selfless action and avoiding forbidden action, and encourages the reader to focus on the present moment and their duty in the present moment rather than worrying about the future or the past.

SEVENTY-FOUR
GYANA KARMA SANYASAYOGA

The Gyana Karma Sanyasayoga is the fourth chapter of the Bhagavad Gita, one of the most important Hindu scriptures. It is also known as the "Yoga of Knowledge and Action" or the "Yoga of Renunciation of Action in Knowledge." This chapter focuses on the concept of detachment from the fruits of one's actions and the importance of knowledge in achieving liberation.

The chapter begins with Arjuna questioning Lord Krishna on the difference between renunciation of action and the path of knowledge. He wants to know which is better and more effective in achieving liberation. Lord Krishna explains that both paths are equally important, but the path of knowledge is superior as it leads to detachment from the fruits of one's actions.

Lord Krishna then goes on to explain the concept of Karma Yoga, which involves performing actions without any attachment to the results. He tells Arjuna that he should perform his duties as a warrior without any attachment to the outcome of the battle. This way, he will be able to perform his duty without being affected by the results.

The Lord then explains that knowledge is the key to detachment from the fruits of action. He explains that one should perform their duties without attachment to the outcome, but they should also seek knowledge of the self to achieve true detachment. By understanding the true nature of the self and realizing that it is distinct from the body and mind, one can achieve a state of complete detachment.

Lord Krishna goes on to explain the importance of performing one's duty without attachment, as it is the path to liberation. He says that even a person who is engaged in action can be free if they perform their duties with detachment. However, a person who renounces action without knowledge is not truly free and cannot achieve liberation.

The chapter concludes with Lord Krishna urging Arjuna to perform his duty as a warrior and not to be swayed by the desire for the fruits of his actions. He tells Arjuna that he should work without attachment and with the knowledge of the self, which is the path to true freedom and liberation.

In summary, the Gyana Karma Sanyasayoga emphasizes the importance of detachment from the fruits of one's actions and the role of knowledge in achieving liberation. It teaches the concept of Karma Yoga, which involves performing one's duty without attachment, and highlights the importance of seeking knowledge of the self to achieve true detachment. The chapter concludes with Lord Krishna urging Arjuna to perform his duty without attachment and with the knowledge of the self, which is the path to true freedom and liberation.

ԖԖԖ

SEVENTY-FIVE
KARMA SANYASA YOGA

Chapter 5 of the Bhagavad Gita, also known as Karma Sanyasayoga, focuses on the concept of renunciation and detachment from material desires. This chapter delves into the essence of true renunciation and how one can attain it.

The chapter begins with Arjuna asking Lord Krishna about the difference between Sanyasa (renunciation) and Tyaga (abandonment). Lord Krishna explains that Sanyasa is the renunciation of actions rooted in desire, while Tyaga is the abandonment of the fruits of actions. He explains that one must have both Sanyasa and Tyaga to achieve liberation from the cycle of birth and death.

Lord Krishna further explains that renunciation does not mean the complete abandonment of all actions. One must perform actions in the world but should not be attached to them. He emphasizes the importance of performing one's duty without attachment to the results, as this leads to a state of equanimity.

Lord Krishna then introduces the concept of the three types of actions: Sattvic, Rajasic, and Tamasic. Sattvic actions are those that are performed without any attachment to the results and are performed as one's duty. Rajasic actions are those performed with attachment to the fruits of actions, while Tamasic actions are those performed with ignorance and delusion.

Lord Krishna explains that those who perform Sattvic actions without attachment to the results are free from the bondage of karma and attain liberation. On the other hand, those who perform Rajasic and Tamasic actions are bound by their actions and suffer in the cycle of birth and death.

The chapter also delves into the concept of sacrifice, which is of two types: the outer sacrifice of material objects and the inner sacrifice of the ego. Lord Krishna explains that the true sacrifice is the inner sacrifice of the ego, as it leads to liberation from the cycle of birth and death.

Furthermore, Lord Krishna stresses the importance of spiritual knowledge and how it leads to liberation. He explains that the one who has attained true knowledge sees the self in all beings and sees all beings in the self. This leads to a state of oneness with the universe and the attainment of eternal bliss.

In conclusion, Chapter 5 of the Bhagavad Gita emphasizes the importance of performing one's duty without attachment to the results, the concept of the three types of actions, the importance of true renunciation, sacrifice, and the attainment of spiritual knowledge. It teaches us that true renunciation does not mean abandoning all actions but performing them without attachment to the results. The chapter inspires us to strive for liberation from the cycle of birth and death by performing Sattvic actions, sacrificing the ego, and attaining spiritual knowledge.

ॐॐॐ

SEVENTY-SIX
ATMA SAMYAMANA YOGA

Chapter 6 of the Bhagavad Gita, also known as the Dhyanayoga or Aatmasamyamyoga, delves into the practice of meditation and self-control as a means to achieve union with the divine. This chapter begins with Arjuna asking Krishna how one can attain steadiness of mind, for he finds it difficult to control his mind and senses.

Krishna explains to Arjuna that the practice of yoga, which includes both action and detachment, is the key to attaining such control. He tells Arjuna that by practicing yoga, one can free oneself from the bondage of attachment and attain a state of equanimity.

Krishna then goes on to explain the importance of meditation in the practice of yoga. He states that one should practice meditation with a focused mind, and should strive to detach oneself from the material world in order to attain a state of spiritual bliss. He describes the importance of controlling the mind, and the role of the senses in this process.

Krishna further elaborates on the importance of renunciation in the path to spiritual enlightenment. He explains that the one who has conquered the senses and the mind is able to attain true happiness and peace, and that those who are attached to the material world are unable to achieve such a state.

The chapter also touches upon the concept of the self, or atma, and how it is related to the body and mind. Krishna explains that the self is separate from the body and the mind, and that one should strive to understand and connect with the self in order to attain true happiness and liberation.

The practice of yoga and meditation, according to Krishna, requires discipline, devotion, and faith. He emphasizes the importance of detachment from the material world, and the need to focus one's mind on the divine. Krishna assures Arjuna that through such practices, one can attain the highest state of consciousness and achieve union with the divine.

In summary, Chapter 6 of the Bhagavad Gita delves into the practice of meditation and self-control as a means to achieve spiritual enlightenment. It emphasizes the importance of detachment from the material world, and the need to control the mind and senses in order to attain a state of equanimity. The chapter also highlights the concept of the self, and the importance of understanding and connecting with it in order to attain true happiness and liberation.

ᐅᐅᐅ

SEVENTY-SEVEN
GYANA VIGYANA YOGA

Chapter 7 of the Bhagavad Gita is known as "Gyana Vigyanayoga" or "The Yoga of Knowledge and Wisdom." This chapter focuses on the nature of the Supreme Being and the importance of developing a relationship with Him through knowledge and devotion.

The chapter begins with Arjuna asking Krishna to explain the nature of those who worship Him with knowledge and those who worship Him with devotion. Krishna responds by saying that both approaches lead to Him, but those who worship Him with knowledge are more steadfast in their devotion. He goes on to explain that He is both the material and spiritual worlds, and that all beings are a part of Him.

Krishna then describes four types of people who do not approach Him: those who are ignorant, those who are attached to material desires, those who seek temporary happiness, and those who are full of false ego. He encourages Arjuna to abandon these qualities and instead focus on Him through devotion and service.

Next, Krishna discusses the importance of understanding His divine nature, which is beyond material comprehension. He explains that through surrender and devotion, one can attain knowledge of His true nature and become free from the cycle of birth and death.

Krishna also emphasizes the importance of spiritual knowledge and the role of a guru in imparting that knowledge. He advises Arjuna to seek a guru who can guide him on the path of spiritual knowledge and liberation.

The chapter concludes with Krishna describing the characteristics of those who have attained spiritual knowledge and are devoted to Him. They are peaceful, self-controlled, compassionate, free from material desires, and devoted to serving others.

In summary, Chapter 7 of the Bhagavad Gita teaches the importance of developing a relationship with the Supreme Being through knowledge and devotion. It emphasizes the need to abandon material desires and false ego, and to seek the guidance of a guru in attaining spiritual knowledge. The chapter encourages the reader to understand the divine nature of the Supreme Being and to become free from the cycle of birth and death through surrender and devotion.

ᬅᬅᬅ

SEVENTY-EIGHT
AKSHARA BRAHMA YOGA

Chapter 8 of the Bhagavad Gita is known as the Akshara Brahmayoga, which means the Yoga of the Imperishable Brahman. This chapter delves deeper into the nature of the ultimate reality and the process of achieving liberation from the cycle of birth and death.

The chapter begins with Arjuna asking Krishna about the nature of the ultimate reality, the process of transcending death, and the path to attaining the Supreme. Krishna responds by saying that one who meditates on the Supreme Being with a focused mind at the time of death attains the Supreme Abode and never returns to the cycle of birth and death.

Krishna then proceeds to explain the concept of the Imperishable Brahman, which is beyond the manifest and unmanifest worlds, and is the ultimate destination of all spiritual seekers. He explains that one who meditates on the Imperishable Brahman with unwavering faith and devotion attains it at the time of death.

Krishna also explains the process of attaining the Supreme Being through the practice of Yoga, which involves focusing the mind on the divine and constantly meditating on the eternal Truth. He emphasizes the importance of detaching oneself from the material world and cultivating a sense of detachment and dispassion towards the pleasures and sorrows of life.

The chapter also includes a description of the different paths that a soul can take after death, depending on their actions and beliefs in life. Krishna explains that those who have devoted themselves to the path of the Supreme Being attain the Supreme Abode, while those who are attached to the material world are born again in the cycle of birth and death.

Krishna concludes the chapter by emphasizing the importance of constantly meditating on the Supreme Being and cultivating a sense of detachment towards the material world in order to attain liberation from the cycle of birth and death.

In summary, Chapter 8 of the Bhagavad Gita delves deeper into the nature of the ultimate reality and the process of achieving liberation from the cycle of birth and death. It emphasizes the importance of focusing the mind on the divine and cultivating a sense of detachment towards the material world in order to attain the Supreme Abode.

ॐॐॐ

SEVENTY-NINE

RAJA VIDYA RAJA GUHYA YOGA

Chapter 9 of the Bhagavad Gita, titled "Raja Vidya Raja Guhyayoga," is a continuation of the previous chapter, delving deeper into the nature of the Supreme Being and the path to attaining Him.

The chapter begins with Lord Krishna revealing that this knowledge is the most profound, most secret, and most sacred of all. He then explains that the Supreme Being, who is both the cause and the effect of all that exists, pervades the entire universe.

Lord Krishna then proceeds to describe the different types of people who worship Him. He explains that those who are devoted to Him with faith and love, those who seek refuge in Him, those who worship Him with knowledge, and those who perform sacrifices for Him are all dear to Him.

Next, Lord Krishna describes the fruits of worshipping Him. He reveals that those who worship Him attain the supreme abode, never to return to the cycle of birth and death. He also explains that those who worship demigods attain temporary results, but those who worship Him attain eternal liberation.

Lord Krishna then emphasizes the importance of surrendering to Him completely, with one's mind always fixed on Him. He assures that He will take care of all the needs of His devotees, who need not worry about anything.

In the latter part of the chapter, Lord Krishna reveals His divine nature as the creator, sustainer, and destroyer of the universe. He states that He is the source of everything, and all things emanate from Him.

Lord Krishna then reveals that by understanding and realizing Him as the Supreme Being, one can attain complete liberation from the cycle of birth and death. He emphasizes the importance of constantly remembering and worshipping Him, with devotion and love.

The chapter ends with Lord Krishna assuring that those who worship Him with love and devotion will always remain in His protection and attain the ultimate goal of life, which is eternal union with Him.

In summary, Chapter 9 of the Bhagavad Gita emphasizes the importance of worshipping the Supreme Being with devotion and love, surrendering to Him completely, and realizing Him as the source of all creation. Lord Krishna reveals His divine nature and assures that those who seek refuge in Him will attain liberation from the cycle of birth and death.

❧❧❧

EIGHTY
VIBHOOTI YOGA

Chapter 10 of the Bhagavad Gita is called "Vibhuti Yoga," which means the "Yoga of Divine Glories." In this chapter, Lord Krishna continues to reveal more about his divine nature and the extent of his powers to Arjuna, who is listening intently.

The chapter begins with Arjuna asking Lord Krishna to reveal more about his divine powers and glories. Lord Krishna responds by saying that he will only reveal a fraction of his powers, as his true nature is infinite and cannot be fully comprehended by mortal beings.

Lord Krishna then begins to describe his divine glories, starting with the fact that he is the source of all beings and all things. He explains that everything in the world comes from him and is sustained by him, and that when the world comes to an end, everything will return to him.

Lord Krishna also reveals that he is the essence of all knowledge, and that all forms of knowledge and wisdom ultimately come from him. He explains that he is the source of all the different qualities and virtues that humans possess, such as courage, generosity, and wisdom.

Lord Krishna goes on to describe his various manifestations in the world, including his presence in the sun and the moon, as well as his ability to control the seasons and the weather. He also describes his presence in all living beings, and how he sustains them through his energy and life force.

As Lord Krishna continues to describe his divine glories, Arjuna becomes overwhelmed by the power and magnitude of his revelations. He falls to his knees and prostrates himself before Lord Krishna, acknowledging him as the ultimate source of all creation and existence.

Lord Krishna concludes the chapter by reassuring Arjuna that he is not revealing his divine nature to intimidate or frighten him, but rather to help him understand the true nature of reality. He urges Arjuna to continue on the path of devotion and surrender to him, in order to attain ultimate liberation from the cycle of birth and death.

Overall, Chapter 10 of the Bhagavad Gita serves as a reminder of the true nature of reality and the role that Lord Krishna plays in the grand scheme of things. Through his divine glories, Lord Krishna reveals the extent of his powers and his presence in all aspects of the world, encouraging Arjuna and all readers to develop a deeper understanding and devotion to him.

ᐅᐅᐅ

EIGHTY-ONE

VISHWAROOPA DARSHANA YOGA

Chapter 11 of the Bhagavad Gita, also known as the Vishvarupa Darshanayoga, is considered one of the most significant and awe-inspiring chapters of the text. In this chapter, Lord Krishna reveals his universal form to Arjuna, giving him a glimpse of the vastness and complexity of the universe, and the power and majesty of the divine.

The chapter begins with Arjuna requesting Lord Krishna to reveal his divine form, so that he may see and worship it. Lord Krishna grants his request, and Arjuna witnesses the divine form of the Lord, which is described in great detail. The Vishvarupa, or universal form, is depicted as a magnificent, multi-headed and multi-limbed entity, with a thousand eyes and countless mouths. Arjuna is filled with wonder and terror at this sight, and Krishna explains to him the significance and symbolism of what he sees.

Krishna explains that the Vishvarupa is the ultimate reality, the source and sustainer of all creation. It represents the cosmic order and the interconnectedness of all things, both visible and invisible. The form is also a manifestation of the divine power and glory, which pervades everything in the universe.

As Arjuna continues to gaze at the Vishvarupa, he sees numerous gods and celestial beings, as well as his own relatives and friends, who have all been consumed by Krishna's divine form. This terrifies Arjuna, and he begs Krishna to return to his original form.

Krishna reassures Arjuna that he need not fear, and that he has revealed his Vishvarupa to him in order to teach him about the true nature of existence. He emphasizes the importance of devotion and surrender to the divine, and explains that true wisdom and liberation can only be attained through complete and unconditional surrender to the will of the Lord.

The chapter concludes with Arjuna expressing his gratitude and awe at having witnessed the divine form of the Lord. He acknowledges that the vision has given him a new understanding of the nature of the universe and the role of the divine in it. He also expresses his willingness to carry out Krishna's commands and to follow his path, knowing that it is the path of truth and righteousness.

In summary, Chapter 11 of the Bhagavad Gita offers a powerful and moving depiction of the divine, as well as a profound insight into the nature of the universe and the interconnectedness of all things. The chapter emphasizes the importance of devotion and surrender to the divine, and encourages the reader to seek a deeper understanding of the true nature of existence. It is a truly awe-inspiring chapter, which has captured the imagination and devotion of countless readers over the centuries.

ॐॐॐ

EIGHTY-TWO
BHAKTI YOGA

Chapter 12 of the Bhagavad Gita is titled "Bhakti Yoga," which means the yoga of devotion. This chapter emphasizes the importance of devotion and surrender to the Divine as the most effective path to attain spiritual enlightenment.

Arjuna begins by asking Krishna about the difference between those who are steadfast in their devotion to the Divine and those who worship the unmanifested. Krishna explains that both paths lead to the Divine, but the path of devotion is considered superior as it is easier to follow and leads to faster progress.

Krishna then goes on to describe the qualities of a true devotee. A true devotee is one who is humble, pure-hearted, unattached, and devoted to the Divine with unwavering faith. The devotee sees the Divine in all beings and serves them with love and compassion. Krishna explains that the path of devotion is not easy, but for those who surrender themselves to the Divine with devotion, the Divine will take care of them.

Krishna further explains that there are different ways of approaching the Divine through devotion, such as worship, offering, and serving. The devotee can choose any of these methods according to their inclination and capacity. But what is essential is that the devotee must surrender their ego and offer everything to the Divine with pure love and devotion.

Krishna then describes the characteristics of a devotee who has attained the highest state of consciousness. Such a devotee is free from all dualities, such as pleasure and pain, and is established in a state of equanimity. They are not attached to anything, including their own body and mind, and have surrendered everything to the Divine. They see the Divine in everything and are always immersed in the bliss of the Divine.

Krishna concludes by saying that the path of devotion is the most accessible and effective way to attain liberation from the cycle of birth and death. It is a path that can be followed by anyone, regardless of their caste, gender, or social status. Krishna urges Arjuna to follow this path of devotion and surrender to the Divine, and he promises that he will protect and guide him always.

In conclusion, Chapter 12 of the Bhagavad Gita emphasizes the importance of devotion and surrender to the Divine as the most effective path to attain spiritual enlightenment. It explains that a true devotee is one who is humble, pure-hearted, unattached, and devoted to the Divine with unwavering faith. The chapter also describes the different ways of approaching the Divine through devotion and the characteristics of a devotee who has attained the highest state of consciousness. The chapter ends with Krishna urging Arjuna to follow the path of devotion and surrender to the Divine, promising that he will protect and guide him always.

ᏇᏇᏇ

EIGHTY-THREE

KSHETRA KSHETRAGYA VIBHAGA YOGA

Chapter 13 of the Bhagavad Gita is titled "Kshetra Kshetragya Vibhagayoga," which means the "Yoga of the Distinction between the Field and the Knower of the Field." This chapter delves into the concept of the "field," which is the physical body, and the "knower of the field," which is the individual soul or consciousness that inhabits the body.

The chapter begins with Arjuna asking Lord Krishna about the difference between the field and the knower of the field. Lord Krishna explains that the body is the field, and the one who knows the body is the knower of the field. He further explains that the knowledge of the field and the knower of the field is the true knowledge.

Lord Krishna then proceeds to describe the nature of the field and the knower of the field. The field is made up of the five elements - earth, water, fire, air, and ether - and the mind, intelligence, and ego. The knower of the field, on the other hand, is the individual soul or consciousness that is present in all beings.

He then describes the different qualities of the knower of the field, such as being unchanging, eternal, and beyond the three modes of material nature - goodness, passion, and ignorance. Lord Krishna also explains that the knower of the field is the true seer, the one who sees everything through the lens of pure consciousness.

Lord Krishna then discusses the importance of knowing the distinction between the field and the knower of the field. He explains that those who are aware of this distinction attain liberation from the cycle of birth and death.

Lord Krishna also explains the concept of the supreme Brahman, which is the ultimate reality, and how it is the cause of all beings. He explains that those who worship the Brahman with devotion and surrender attain enlightenment and liberation.

The chapter concludes with Lord Krishna exhorting Arjuna to know the true nature of the field and the knower of the field, and to realize that the individual soul is distinct from the body. He encourages Arjuna to develop the qualities of humility, simplicity, and non-violence, and to devote himself to the worship of the supreme Brahman.

In summary, Chapter 13 of the Bhagavad Gita provides a deep understanding of the nature of the field and the knower of the field, and emphasizes the importance of realizing the distinction between the two. The chapter also emphasizes the importance of devotion and surrender to the ultimate reality, the supreme Brahman, for attaining liberation and enlightenment.

ॐॐॐ

EIGHTY-FOUR

GUNATRAYA VIBHAGA YOGA

Chapter 14 of the Bhagavad Gita is known as the "Gunatraya Vibhagayoga" or "Yoga of the Three Qualities". In this chapter, Lord Krishna explains the three modes of material nature, their characteristics, and how they influence human behavior and consciousness.

Lord Krishna begins by stating that all living entities in this world are under the influence of the three modes of material nature - sattva, rajas, and tamas. These modes are the basis of all material existence and are responsible for the different actions and reactions of living beings. He further explains that the mode of goodness or sattva is pure and illuminating, the mode of passion or rajas is characterized by intense desire and attachment, and the mode of ignorance or tamas is characterized by laziness, lethargy, and ignorance.

Lord Krishna explains that those who are situated in the mode of goodness are able to see things as they are and are not influenced by material desires or attachments. They are free from the dualities of happiness and distress, and are able to maintain equanimity in all situations. Those situated in the mode of passion are always striving for more material possessions and are often driven by a sense of competition and ego. Those situated in the mode of ignorance are unable to see things clearly and are often deluded by false perceptions.

Lord Krishna then explains how the three modes of material nature influence our actions, thoughts, and consciousness. He explains that those situated in the mode of goodness are able to perform selfless actions that are free from personal desires or attachments, and are not affected by the reactions of their actions. Those situated in the mode of passion perform actions that are driven by personal desire and attachment, and are bound by the reactions of their actions. Those situated in the mode of ignorance are unable to perform actions properly and often end up causing harm to themselves and others.

Lord Krishna concludes the chapter by stating that those who transcend the three modes of material nature by practicing devotional service to Him are able to attain ultimate liberation and eternal happiness. By surrendering all actions and desires to Him, one is able to overcome the influence of the material modes and achieve true spiritual realization.

In summary, Chapter 14 of the Bhagavad Gita teaches us about the three modes of material nature and their influence on human behavior and consciousness. By understanding these modes, we are able to become more self-aware and make conscious choices that are in alignment with our spiritual goals. Ultimately, the chapter reminds us that true liberation and eternal happiness can only be attained by surrendering ourselves to the Divine and practicing devotion to Him.

ॐॐॐ

EIGHTY-FIVE

PURUSHOTTAMA YOGA

Chapter 15 of the Bhagavad Gita is titled "Purushottamayoga," which means the yoga of the Supreme Being. In this chapter, Lord Krishna explains to Arjuna the nature of the Supreme Being and the path to reach Him.

Lord Krishna begins by describing the world tree, which has roots above and branches below, symbolizing the eternal nature of the Supreme Being. He then reveals that the embodied soul is a part of the Supreme Being and can attain eternal happiness by surrendering to Him.

Krishna explains that the material world is temporary and full of suffering, while the spiritual world is eternal and full of bliss. The Supreme Being is the source of all material and spiritual worlds and can only be realized by surrendering to Him with devotion and performing selfless actions.

Krishna then describes the two types of beings in the world, the perishable and the imperishable. The perishable beings are those who identify with their body and mind and are subject to birth and death. The imperishable beings are those who have realized their true nature as the Supreme Being and are free from the cycle of birth and death.

Krishna urges Arjuna to strive for the realization of the Supreme Being, who is beyond the perishable and imperishable, and by doing so, attain the ultimate goal of life. He emphasizes the importance of cultivating knowledge, detachment, and devotion to reach the Supreme Being.

Krishna also explains the concept of the "supreme person," who is the cause of creation, maintenance, and destruction of the universe. He is the ultimate object of worship and the goal of all spiritual practices.

In the latter part of the chapter, Krishna explains how one can attain the Supreme Being by meditating on Him and practicing detachment from the material world. He emphasizes the importance of focusing the mind on the Supreme Being and surrendering to Him completely.

Krishna concludes the chapter by saying that those who follow this path of devotion and knowledge will attain the Supreme Being and will never fall down from that position. He urges Arjuna to take up this path and strive for the realization of the Supreme Being.

Overall, Chapter 15 of the Bhagavad Gita emphasizes the importance of surrendering to the Supreme Being and cultivating knowledge, detachment, and devotion to reach Him. It provides a clear understanding of the nature of the Supreme Being and the path to attain Him.

ॐॐॐ

EIGHTY-SIX

DAIVASURA SAMPAD VIBHAGA YOGA

Chapter 16 of the Bhagavad Gita is titled "Daivasura Sampad Vibhagayoga," which means the "Yoga of distinguishing between divine and demoniac qualities." This chapter is important because it emphasizes the distinction between the divine qualities that lead to spiritual growth and the demoniac qualities that lead to spiritual decline.

In this chapter, Lord Krishna explains to Arjuna that there are two types of people in the world: those who possess divine qualities and those who possess demoniac qualities. The divine qualities include fearlessness, purity of mind, steadfastness in spiritual knowledge, charity, self-control, sacrifice, and study of the Vedas. On the other hand, the demoniac qualities include pride, arrogance, conceit, anger, harshness, ignorance, and hypocrisy.

Lord Krishna warns Arjuna that those who possess demoniac qualities are doomed to a life of misery and suffering. They are constantly driven by selfish desires and are unable to find true happiness or contentment in life. In contrast, those who possess divine qualities are able to achieve spiritual growth and ultimately attain liberation from the cycle of birth and death.

Lord Krishna goes on to explain that the demoniac qualities are born from lust and attachment to the material world. Those who are driven by these desires become entangled in a web of illusion and are unable to see the true nature of the world. They are constantly chasing after pleasure and material possessions, but are never truly satisfied.

In contrast, those who possess divine qualities are able to transcend the material world and realize the true nature of the self. They understand that the material world is impermanent and full of suffering, and they strive to attain spiritual knowledge and self-realization. Through this process, they are able to find true happiness and contentment in life.

Lord Krishna concludes this chapter by urging Arjuna to cultivate the divine qualities and avoid the demoniac qualities. He emphasizes the importance of spiritual knowledge and the need to overcome attachment to the material world. By doing so, one can attain true happiness and ultimately achieve liberation from the cycle of birth and death.

Overall, Chapter 16 of the Bhagavad Gita serves as a reminder of the importance of cultivating divine qualities and avoiding demoniac qualities. It emphasizes the need for spiritual growth and the pursuit of self-realization as a means to achieve true happiness and fulfillment in life.

ॐॐॐ

EIGHTY-SEVEN
SHRADDHATRAYA VIBHAGA YOGA

Chapter 17 of the Bhagavad Gita, known as the Shraddhatraya Vibhagayoga, delves into the concept of faith and how it affects one's actions and spiritual journey. The chapter is divided into three sections, each representing one of the three types of faith - sattvic, rajasic, and tamasic.

The chapter begins with Arjuna asking Lord Krishna about the difference between sattvic, rajasic, and tamasic faith, and how each affects one's actions. Lord Krishna explains that one's faith is reflected in their actions and that all actions are influenced by the quality of one's faith.

The first section of the chapter discusses sattvic faith, which is characterized by purity, truthfulness, and devotion. Lord Krishna explains that those with sattvic faith worship the gods, perform austerities, and offer charity with a pure heart, without expecting anything in return. Such actions are performed without attachment or desire for material benefits, and are solely for the purpose of spiritual purification and elevation.

The second section discusses rajasic faith, which is characterized by passion, desire, and attachment to material things. Those with rajasic faith worship the gods for material gains and perform austerities with the aim of gaining power and fame. Their actions are motivated by their desires and attachment to material things, and they are often carried out with arrogance and ego.

The third and final section discusses tamasic faith, which is characterized by ignorance, laziness, and delusion. Those with tamasic faith worship ghosts and spirits, perform austerities with the aim of causing harm to others, and offer charity with the intention of showing off or gaining something in return. Their actions are driven by their ignorance and lack of spiritual knowledge, and they are often harmful to themselves and others.

Lord Krishna then explains that one's faith is not fixed and can be changed with effort and determination. He advises Arjuna to cultivate sattvic faith by surrendering to the divine and performing actions without attachment or desire for material gains. He also warns against the dangers of tamasic and rajasic faith, which lead to spiritual decline and suffering.

The chapter concludes with Lord Krishna emphasizing the importance of faith in spiritual growth and liberation. He advises Arjuna to have unwavering faith and to surrender to the divine will, which will ultimately lead to spiritual enlightenment and freedom from the cycle of birth and death.

In summary, Chapter 17 of the Bhagavad Gita explores the concept of faith and its impact on one's actions and spiritual journey. It highlights the importance of cultivating sattvic faith, which is characterized by purity, truthfulness, and devotion, while warning against the dangers of rajasic and tamasic faith. Lord Krishna emphasizes the importance of unwavering faith and surrender to the divine will as a means to attain spiritual liberation.

॥ ॐ ॐ ॐ ॥

• 191 •

EIGHTY-EIGHT
MOKSHA SANYASA YOGA

Chapter 18 of the Bhagavad Gita, also known as Moksha Sanyasayoga, is the final chapter of the text. It is believed to have been delivered by Lord Krishna to Arjuna when they were in the midst of the Kurukshetra war. The chapter focuses on the concept of renunciation and liberation, and how one can achieve these goals by performing their duties in a detached and selfless manner.

The chapter begins with Arjuna asking Lord Krishna to explain the difference between Sanyasa (renunciation) and Tyaga (abandonment). Lord Krishna explains that Sanyasa is the renunciation of all actions that are motivated by desire or attachment, whereas Tyaga is the abandonment of all actions without regard to their consequences. He also explains that the ultimate goal of both Sanyasa and Tyaga is the same, which is to attain liberation from the cycle of birth and death.

Lord Krishna then proceeds to explain the four different types of people who practice these two paths. He explains that those who practice Sanyasa with the aim of renouncing their desires and attachments are known as the Sankhya Yogis. Those who practice Tyaga out of fear or due to their inability to perform their duties are known as the Rajasic Tyagis. Those who perform their duties with the expectation of rewards or recognition are known as the Tamasic Tyagis. Finally, those who perform their duties without any attachment or desire for the fruits of their actions are known as the Satvic Tyagis.

Lord Krishna emphasizes that the path of Sanyasa is not for everyone and that one must perform their duties in a manner that is appropriate for their individual nature and capabilities. He explains that each individual is born with a particular set of qualities and tendencies, known as Gunas, which influence their actions and behavior. He then proceeds to explain the three Gunas - Satva, Rajas, and Tamas - and how they manifest in different people and situations.

Lord Krishna goes on to explain that one can achieve liberation by performing their duties in a selfless manner, without attachment to the fruits of their actions. He explains that one must act according to their Swadharma, or their individual duty, without being influenced by their desires, attachments, or fears. He stresses that one must not give up their duties or responsibilities, but must instead perform them with dedication and devotion to God.

Lord Krishna also explains the importance of surrendering one's actions and their fruits to God, and the role of devotion in achieving liberation. He explains that one can attain liberation by practicing devotion to God through various means, such as meditation, prayer, and offering of one's actions to God.

The chapter concludes with Lord Krishna summarizing the main teachings of the Bhagavad Gita and urging Arjuna to reflect on them and make a decision. He explains that he has revealed the knowledge of the Bhagavad Gita to Arjuna out of love and compassion for him, and that it is up to Arjuna to decide whether to accept it or not.

In conclusion, Chapter 18 of the Bhagavad Gita emphasizes the importance of performing one's duties in a selfless and detached manner, without attachment to the fruits of one's actions. It stresses the importance of understanding one's nature and following one's Swadharma, or individual duty, without being influenced by desires or fears. It also highlights the importance of surrendering one's actions and their fruits to God and practicing devotion as a means of achieving liberation from the cycle of birth and death.

ᐅᐅᐅ

RAMCHARITMANAS

EIGHTY-NINE
RAMCHARITMANAS

Ramcharitmanas is a devotional text in Hindi, composed by the 16th-century Indian poet Goswami Tulsidas. It is one of the most popular and widely-read works of Hindi literature and is a retelling of the epic Ramayana.

The Ramayana is a story of the triumph of good over evil, and the Ramcharitmanas follows the same narrative arc. The story revolves around Lord Rama, the seventh avatar of Lord Vishnu, and his wife Sita. Rama is considered an ideal man and an embodiment of dharma, or righteousness, while Sita is a symbol of purity and devotion.

The Ramcharitmanas is divided into seven kands or books, each of which narrates a different part of the story. The first book, Balakand, describes the birth of Rama and his childhood, while the second book, Ayodhyakand, describes his marriage to Sita and his exile from the kingdom of Ayodhya. The third book, Aranyakand, narrates Rama's journey through the forest and his encounter with various sages and demons. The fourth book, Kishkindhakand, narrates the story of Rama's alliance with Hanuman, the monkey god, and his efforts to rescue Sita from the demon king Ravana. The fifth book, Sundarkand, describes Hanuman's journey to Lanka and his encounter with Ravana. The sixth book, LankaKand, describes the final battle between Rama and Ravana, and the seventh book, UttarKand, describes Rama's coronation and his return to Ayodhya.

The Ramcharitmanas is written in the chaupai and doha forms of poetry, which consist of four-line and two-line stanzas, respectively. The language is simple and easy to understand, making it accessible to a wide audience. The text is also full of devotional hymns and songs, which are popular among devotees of Lord Rama.

The Ramcharitmanas is not only a literary masterpiece but also a spiritual guide for millions of Hindus. It teaches the importance of dharma, devotion, and service to others. The text is also an important source of inspiration for many poets, musicians, and artists.

In summary, the Ramcharitmanas is a devotional text that tells the story of Lord Rama and his triumph over evil. It is a masterpiece of Hindi literature and an important source of spiritual guidance for millions of Hindus.

ꕤꕤꕤ

HANUMAN CHALISA

NINETY

HANUMAN CHALISA

Hanuman Chalisa is a devotional hymn dedicated to Lord Hanuman, one of the most revered deities in Hinduism. It is a popular prayer recited by millions of devotees worldwide, especially during auspicious occasions such as Hanuman Jayanti and Tuesdays. The prayer consists of forty verses, each describing the glory and greatness of Lord Hanuman.

The Hanuman Chalisa was composed by the famous poet and saint Tulsidas, who lived in the 16th century. According to legend, Tulsidas was a devotee of Lord Rama and had a vision of Hanuman, who inspired him to write the hymn. It is believed that reciting the Hanuman Chalisa with devotion can bring blessings and remove obstacles from one's life.

The prayer begins with an invocation to Lord Hanuman, praising his strength, wisdom, and devotion to Lord Rama. The first verse reads:

"Jai Hanuman gyan gun sagar,
Jai Kapis tihun lok ujagar"

Translation: "Hail Hanuman, the ocean of knowledge and virtues, hail the monkey god who illuminates the three worlds."

The next few verses describe Hanuman's role in the Ramayana, an ancient Hindu epic that tells the story of Lord Rama's journey to rescue his wife Sita from the demon king Ravana. Hanuman is depicted as a loyal and devoted servant of Lord Rama, who uses his strength and intelligence to overcome the challenges faced during the journey.

The hymn also describes Hanuman's physical appearance, such as his powerful build, sparkling eyes, and flowing tail. It is said that each verse of the Hanuman Chalisa has a specific meaning and significance, highlighting various aspects of Lord Hanuman's greatness.

The Hanuman Chalisa also emphasizes the importance of devotion to Lord Rama and Lord Hanuman, and the power of their blessings in overcoming difficulties and achieving success in life. The prayer concludes with a plea to Hanuman to bless the devotee with strength, wisdom, and devotion.

The Hanuman Chalisa has been widely popularized in various forms, including music and art. It is often recited in temples and homes, as well as during devotional gatherings and festivals. Many people also carry a copy of the prayer with them for protection and blessings.

In summary, the Hanuman Chalisa is a devotional hymn dedicated to Lord Hanuman, composed by Tulsidas in the 16th century. It praises Hanuman's strength, wisdom, and devotion to Lord Rama, and describes his role in the Ramayana. The prayer emphasizes the power of devotion and the blessings of Lord Hanuman in overcoming difficulties and achieving success in life.

ᐅᐅᐅ

References And Citations

This book has been created by referencing various websites on the internet, including Wikipedia in order to gather valuable information and data. In addition to online sources, this book also draws upon the author's own research and includes references to relevant books in the library. By combining a variety of sources, this book provides a comprehensive and well-researched account of the subject matter. The author has taken care to ensure that all information presented is accurate and properly cited to give credit to the original sources.

Although every effort has been made to ensure the accuracy and completeness of the information presented in this book, human errors may still occur. If any reader discovers an error or omission in this book, I respectfully welcome their feedback and encourage them to bring it to my attention. Such feedback is valuable to me, and I will take all necessary steps to correct any errors and improve the content of this book in future editions. Thank you for your understanding and support.

|| LOKAHA SAMASTAHA SUKHINO BHAVANTU ||

❤❤❤